To
H...
you &
with love Daph
xc

# BANANA SKINS ON THE SPIRITUAL PATH

## by Daphne Francis

Bright Pen

British Library Cataloguing Publication Data.
A catalogue record for this book is available from the
British Library

ISBN: 978-0-7552-1488-4

Authors OnLine Ltd
19 The Cinques
Gamlingay, Sandy
Bedfordshire SG19 3NU
England

This book is also available in e-book format, details of
which are available at www.authorsonline.co.uk

# CONTENTS

1. Yippee !! Divine abundance is for me !!          1

2. Healing crisis at creeping snake camp          14

3. A trip up the left-hand path?          31

4. Tantric mysteries revealed          39

5. Right-on? On the right hand path          58

6. The master plan exposed          88

7. Rebirth into reality          106

8. Chapter the last - or is it?          119

# CHAPTER 1

## YIPPEE!! DIVINE ABUNDANCE IS FOR ME!!

Flowing just wasn't. In fact, she was feeling totally blocked. All around her, the others enrolled in the Prosperity Consciousness Seminar seemed to be absorbing the new ideas effortlessly. As Aurora, looking cool, poised and ultra-chic in her Armani clothes (a decollete stretch velvet jacket with cotton and lycra striped stirrup leggings) introduced them to the notion that there is an inexhaustible supply in the universe, Flowing was grimly aware of the problem gnawing away in the back reaches of her brain. How was she to come up with £36.25 for her share of the electricity bill, let alone the £200 for this weekend? She had been crazy to come along to the Centre for Divine Abundance. Here she was wasting £10 an hour's worth of wisdom by not concentrating. Really, she must get her head around this. She screwed up all her energy and tuned in on Aurora.

Aurora had soft, wispy curls, eager penetrating eyes and a confident relaxed style. Her pert little outfit suggested money, but money with a difference. On her heart-chakra was a badge which, every so often, lit up (yes, really) in rainbow colours - it read - 'I am a miracle in the game of life'. The pulsating rhythm of the light riveted the eyes of those gathered round her.

The constraints of the jacket presented her breasts as soft, bouncy, womanly flesh, yet with a firmness of purpose, a fine example of the integration of masculine and feminine energies. Her very nipples seemed straining to probe the far mysteries of the universe.

For Aurora was dedicated to higher consciousness and that brought with it, it seemed, trails of riches. 'Prosperity, or lack of it', came from her perfectly lip-sticked, faintly moist lips, 'is an outer expression of the ideas in your head. If we do not accept the idea that we deserve to prosper, then even when abundance falls in our laps, we will refuse it somehow.' Then followed an elucidating example of some former client of Aurora's for whom the creeping recognition of his self-worth had brought in an unexpected windfall of £500 from the death of some obscure relative. He had exclaimed 'Wow, I just don't believe it' and sure enough, next week, he had fallen headlong downstairs, been laid up for several weeks, and lost the equivalent of £720 in wages. He just wasn't ready to live with that amount of abundance, it seemed. He just hadn't been open to receiving. Now Flowing was to be given an opportunity to avoid such pitfalls. For the next hour before lunch, she was to pair up with another, and they were to make affirmations- statements about how much they deserved love, how beautiful they were, how they were capable of attracting what they needed into their lives. Whom should she choose?

She glanced surreptitiously round the room. Whom would she feel least self-conscious with? Who wouldn't notice the incipient hole in her shoe, gaping evidence of slob-consciousness? Her gaze came to rest on James, a young, bespectacled and rather dilapidated-looking Primary School teacher. James had earlier distinguished himself in Flowing's eyes by managing to elicit from Aurora a response that for an instant semi-cracked the veneer of calm confidence. James had rather hesitantly queried that surely money was created by hard work, and, in our more affluent societies, much of our wealth came, not from the thoughts in our heads, but from the blood, sweat and toil of the third world. Flowing had detected a slight suggestion of frostiness in Aurora's nevertheless casual reply. James' position, it seemed, represented old-age limited thinking. The sooner he let go of those outmoded concepts, the sooner he would enjoy the bounty that Aurora's ideas obviously brought to herself. As everyone turned to focus on him, James had turned a shade close to beetroot and closed his mouth. Yes, Flowing thought, James was in no position to judge her down-at-heel shoes. He was obviously operating in a more old-age mode than herself.

So she walked over to James and they sat opposite each other on comfy cushions. Aurora demonstrated the approved procedure. With a very keen student, Marianne, her eyes emanating undeniable warmth, she held Marianne's hands, and, radiating one hundred percent certainty, stated 'You are a most beautiful being. Repeat this back to me.' There was a strained silence. Meanwhile Flowing contemplated Marianne in all her glory. The recent perm couldn't conceal the rather pronounced bald patches, presumably caused by nerves. Her complexion was blotchy and further coloured by an over-zealous application of rather lurid make-up. Her nose veered menacingly to one side of her face and her chin to the other. Her body tone was reminiscent of a sack of mature potatoes rather past the sell-by-date. Obviously, Flowing mused, Aurora had picked Marianne to demonstrate that, with mind-control, anything was possible. But was it?

Marianne seemed, for all her keenness, on the point of mutiny. 'Oh no, Aurora' she wailed. 'It's not true. Why, I'm almost bald.' A tear started to trickle down her cheek. Aurora's composure increased. 'Oh yes, Marianne. You have the most lovely head of hair. Repeat after me - "I have a most lovely head of hair". Try it. It really works.' Marianne sobbed convulsively, squirmed self-consciously and tried, manfully, to come out with her self-blessing. 'That's great' assured Aurora. 'Again, with conviction.' She kept on at Marianne with the zest of an excited spaniel harrying a pheasant into flight. 'Yes. Yes, I have a lovely head of hair' she screamed. 'I know it. I feel it. It's true.' Aurora beamed. 'Great, and that's only a beginning. Now get to work, you others. Marianne and I will continue affirming her beauty.'

The next hour was pure agony for Flowing and James seemed equally tormented. 'Yes' he would mumble. 'I am a wonderfully attractive man. I am a wonderfully attractive man. I easily attract women into my life.' Flowing valiantly attempted to mirror

Aurora's firm handling of her partner's obvious self-doubt and reticence. 'Yes. it's true' she applauded. The sweat was pouring off James. He looked distinctly less attractive than he had at the start of the workshop, thought Flowing, and that wasn't saying much. But she mustn't betray any glimpse of her true feelings. Everything, everything, including James, was just perfect the way it was. And now it was her turn to change her thought-programmes.

How she got through the next ridiculous half-hour, she didn't know. But she did. And didn't she feel just a little better about herself? Flowing's heart leapt. Perhaps the new mind-set was taking a grip. Suddenly, the spectre of the unpaid electricity bill, waiting for her in her dull little room, loosened its grip a little. Perhaps the divine process would pay it off after all. A sneaky after-thought kicked her down into the pits again, however. Probably she was feeling better because the prospect of the lunch-break freed her from the impossible burden of aspiring to be perfect.

Over lunch, of sprouted beans and seeds of all descriptions with a paradoxically sickly chocolate cake, Flowing had a chance to examine others in the workshop. What had, at first impression, seemed a cohesive group of eagerly positive students, on closer scrutiny, struggling to eat assorted sprouts with decorum and seeming enjoyment, turned out to be an assembly of rather anxiety-ridden individuals who, like herself, were clutching at straws, or, in this case, sprouts. Not much was exchanged between them about the morning's proceedings as they munched stolidly through the healthy fare, then squelched their way messily through the cake. All too soon, the lunch-break was over and the group settled back into a full afternoon's session on opening themselves to life's cornucopia.

First of all Aurora regaled them with the details of her life-story. Surely, if she could make it, anyone else in the group could. For there could be no crowning her story of childhood miseries - the loss of her drug-dealing father at age two, butchered bloodily before her infant eyes, then a violent drunken step-father, a rape at age five by an uncle, constant battling and poverty. Moreover, she contracted polio at age seven and had to heave herself around on unsightly callipers through the self-conscious years of adolescence. Aurora had manifested the most appalling suffering - why, even at a children's Christmas party, hobbling as fast as she could, she was the one left out at the end when Santa ran out of glitteringly-wrapped parcels - such was her low self-esteem.

The catalogue of disasters continued through a further rape, drugs, abusive lovers until one fateful day, Aurora's Higher Self guided her to the new teachings. And she began to learn how she had attracted all these harrowing experiences to herself. She had chosen her inadequate parents to teach herself valuable karmic lessons and she had now finally chosen to manifest a different reality for herself. She now realised she was one hundred-percent responsible for everything that happened to her. She described how her low self-esteem and fear had set her up for rape, not once in her life, but twice. It took her many years, she confessed, to truly accept her total responsibility for such outrages. But now that she had stopped blaming her misery on others or on the system, she was able to step right out to take charge of her life and make of it all that she wanted.

And it seemed that she could now manifest anything she desired. The cruel violent lovers were vibed away and sensitive handsome studs were magnetically drawn by her new signals. The days of penury were long past and she now lived in comfort. She made it a habit to kiss every bill as it came in. It was a sign that out there in the universe, somebody believed she was worthy of credit. All in all, Aurora beamed triumphantly, if I, with my rotten history, can create my own success story, then of course so can you.

Flowing heard this sharing by Aurora with mixed feelings, firstly, of relief, that the dazzling Aurora's sordid antecedents demonstrated that she was actually of the same flawed human species as others in the room, then next of awe, that even with such a classically dreadful start, Aurora had not landed up a down-and-out whiner, but was one of life's winners. Finally, Flowing felt daunted. How could <u>she</u> convert her rather shabby life into such a splendid wholesome model? Through her mind flashed snatches of her past, her dull clerk of a father, their greasy little Bradford semi, her uptight and narrow-minded mother, her escape from all this to University, her dropping-out and landing up living with a group of women, drifting from one thing to another, always short of a penny, and attracting one callous creep after another. It seemed a far remove from Aurora's glamorous and love-filled existence. Could she make such changes? Did she, in fact, want to? Was Aurora real? or was she just pulling the wool over her own eyes, and those of others?

Surveying Aurora's glowing smiling face, Flowing concluded that Aurora was for real. A thought, however, was nagging at her mind. Through all her outpourings, Aurora had not once mentioned issues of class or the fact that, as a woman, she was more likely to attract rape. And was she implying that all the poor and suffering in the world could easily lift themselves from squalor? Did Aurora think all of human misery was self-imposed by separate individuals and that the ills of society were all the product of the negative thinking of individuals? Flowing's mind began to reel and baulk. Surely this was going a bit far.

It seemed others in the room were also feeling slightly uneasy. There was a shifting of bottoms, a clearing of throats. Finally, James worked himself up to another question. Glowering at her through his thick lenses, he growled at Aurora. 'Are you implying that the Ethiopians single-handedly brought their own suffering on themselves?' Aurora hesitated before replying - 'Well, you see, nobody needs to suffer poverty. As I have said, there is plenty of divine abundance for everyone. Some souls have yet to realise this truth. This is not to blame them - rather to have compassion and... .' James would not let her finish. He leapt to his feet, snatched his cushion and hurled it blindly across the room. It impacted heavily with a shrine that Aurora had built in a corner, sending flowers, candles and incense to the four directions. The atmosphere was electric. James was snorting convulsively. 'This is fascism' he blurted out, ' I am staying no longer.' And with an ugly and violent leer, he bolted out of the room, slamming the door. The force of his departure caused a tasteful picture to slide slowly down the wall and smash to smithereens.

There was a pregnant pause. Everyone looked to Aurora. Aurora, however, looked calm and unruffled - 'Our teachings are so powerful, you see, that they can cause strong reactions in others. James isn't ready at the moment to embrace change. Let's have a moment of silence and think positive, healing thoughts about him. Let's visualise James smiling and happy and surrounded by divine plenty.' The room relaxed. Certainly this was an easier and more edifying vision than the recent glimpse of an enraged and out-of-control man.

Discreetly, after the moments of silence, Aurora slipped round the room, putting to rights the signs of disruption caused by James' abrupt withdrawal. Soothing sounds of the seashore drifted from the sound-system and the tranquillising odour of sandalwood incense wafted away any remnant of jangled nerves. 'When it comes down to it' Aurora warbled, 'it's all about what sort of person you want to be, unhappy, angry and blaming others, or calmly loving, even those whom it seems have hurt us. For after all, when I <u>really</u> look at my poor mother and father, they too had so much pain as kids - I was just the victim of other victims. It's when we stop blaming and forgive, that real changes can happen. I like to visualise my Mum and Dad as little toddlers reaching out to me for hugs, then I place that image in my heart and love it.' 'A far cry from James' undiscerning anger' thought Flowing - 'It's so much easier and nicer to be compassionate and understanding.' The room relaxed still further. 'And now' Aurora announced 'it's time to meet with crystal energy. I think you're all ready'.

The rest of the day drifted by comparatively easily after the rigours of the start. Each member of the group was given a sparkling crystal from Aurora, a sign surely that they were beginning to manifest beauty in their lives. They were told of the power of crystals to amplify vibrations and how they had been used by ancient cultures as spiritual tools. The crystals Aurora had given them had been specially charged up by members of the Centre for Divine Abundance to help manifest positive and prosperous energies. Aurora encouraged them to sleep with them under their pillows. They were also to each bring a small gift next morning to exchange with another.

By next morning, the group energy was indeed beginning to lift. The morning was spent in further work in releasing past fear of abundance. Each worked on recounting their past histories with money, their family myths, all the old patterns that locked them still into lack. They all seemed to share very much the same story with minor variations - of daily, dismal childhood indoctrinations, beliefs drummed into their naturally rich souls - that money didn't grow on trees, that it was the root of all evil and that once poor, always poor. To replace such limiting philosophies, Aurora, sparkling with delight, revealed to them the new economics. Aurora's laws of supply and demand certainly were one in the eye to those of the dismal science. Demand comes first, and money has a way of coming to where it is needed - why, even the poorest family can almost always get together the money for a funeral. If people really want something, they can manifest it by the power of their thoughts. As they expanded their consciousness and conceived of more, then more would come into their lives. It was like a cosmic bank. Mental deposits needed to be made through meditation and positive affirmations to increase one's awareness of one's ability to create. There was no excuse for whingers to say that they couldn't afford to come to this or that workshop - if they were really meant to come, the means would be made available. Aurora had many a tale to tell of minor money miracles enabling previously down-and-out clients to manifest money for just the workshop they needed to increase their understanding. Why, Judith at present attending this weekend had really been at a loss as to how to get money to come and then she had the bright idea of raising two hundred pounds by selling a gold locket given to her by her great - grandmother.

Flowing absorbed all this diligently. It did cross her mind, however, that the miracles recounted by Aurora mostly, like Judith's, seemed to hinge on having hidden assets to fall back on. But then, she told herself, perhaps Judith and the other miracle-workers had chosen comfortably-off great-grandparents in order to help them on their way to higher consciousness. How was she to come up with the goodies, not having had the awareness to incarnate into a comfortably-off family? Was there any hope for the likes of her? She at last dared to give voice to her self-doubts. Aurora rushed to her with a warm embrace. 'Now sit, Flowing, open your arms out and say "I am open and receptive to all the abundance in the universe."' She prescribed a dose of this every day for a month to build up Flowing's sense of self-worth. She guaranteed that money would flow towards Flowing, not only for the electricity bill, but for all the other steps she needed to take to embrace higher consciousness. Such was her effusive conviction, Flowing felt her doubts melt. Of course, it worked for Aurora, it could work for her.

Next, they formed a circle and each person had to form a mental image to represent all the obstacles to their prosperity. Evincing a yell, they had to cast it into the middle to banish the shackling concept for ever. Yelling wildly, everyone got off on that. 'My self-hatred' shrieked Marianne. 'My penny-pinching' shouted another. 'My electricity bill' wailed Flowing, casting it mentally, with all her energy, away from her. She felt totally purged and almost free from all her past fears. From now on, she was going forward into abundance. She now realised her up-tightness over money stemmed directly from her anxiety-ridden mother. She no longer needed to hold on to such stuff. Her life was for enjoying.

She enjoyed her lunch. And so did all the others. And the afternoon whizzed by on a real high. They composed chants affirming their own openness to life. They sang them and danced joyously. Marianne looked positively transformed, scarcely recognisable from yesterday's human wreck. They all exchanged gifts to take from the workshop and to remind them to continue with their affirmations. Flowing received a sterling-silver angel earring - she felt truly blessed. She was looking forward to getting back into the real world and putting her new ideas into practice.

The first thing she would do, she decided, would be to get rid of that poster in her bedroom. It showed a starving black woman carrying a load of firewood on her head and a bag-of-bones of a child in her arms. It read 'Half of the world's population are women, yet women own less than one hundredth of the world's property.' Looking at that every day could only bring her down. She visualised a new poster in its place, one showing a hazy waterfall in a tranquil pine forest. Her mind began to think over other changes she needed to make in her life. After a warm round of hugs of farewell, Flowing left the Centre for Divine Abundance, £200 poorer but feeling she owned the world.

# CHAPTER 2

# HEALING CRISIS AT CREEPING SNAKE CAMP

Suffused with her new sense of plenty, Flowing decided in the course of the next few days to set off soon for a week in the country at a Healing Camp. She had seen it advertised at the Centre for Divine Abundance at £150 one week in the restful country in Somerset, with hot-tubs, sweat-lodges, workshops on herbs, astrology, reflexology, the lot, in an atmosphere dedicated to harmony and higher awareness. At the time, £150 had seemed a bit steep, but with her new sense of reality, Flowing felt she deserved a bit of a break. She was beginning to appreciate her true self-worth.

And things in the house weren't working too smoothly. Liz and Alice hadn't been too impressed by some of the changes she had been making. In fact, they had been positively hostile. Alice had salvaged the poster she had discarded and had stuck it prominently on the bathroom door. Flowing could no longer relax in the bath without having to contemplate the hideous misery head-on. Liz, pettily to Flowing's mind, had kept harping on about the money she owed for the electricity bill. She hadn't seemed at all satisfied with Flowing's assurances that if she, Liz, would just relax about it, and trust the flow, she would see that the money for the bill was on its way. In fact, she had snorted contemptuously and stamped her foot. Moreover, she was insensitively refusing to call her by her new name and kept calling her Linda. She hadn't been Linda for some weeks now, since her first initiation into New Age living at a weekend workshop at the Self Centre.

The energies around her living companions, Flowing concluded, were getting distinctly unharmonious. Perhaps it was time for her to find herself a different space, one more in tune with her new way of being. A week at the camp would give her the chance she needed to work out possible options.

But how was she to manifest the money to pay for her share of the electricity bill, honour Aurora's trust of her credit-worthiness - the £200 owing to the Centre for Divine Abundance and pay for the Healing Camp? All in all, the sum she needed amounted to nearly £400. Every night, she dutifully slept with her charged-up crystal under her pillow. Every morning, she zealously seated herself facing her window and chanted 'I am open and receptive to all the Good and Abundance in the Universe.' Her first sessions had proved painfully cold but she soldiered on, swaddled in blankets. After six days of intensive concentration, her faith in the new methods had reached breaking-point. She sat grimly contemplating her shoes, from one of which her toe prominently protruded. She had just heard that the Bike Collective, where she had been working for a small wage, was having to close. Despair began to percolate her thoughts, why, things seemed to be getting worse, not better, she frowned. She had failed Aurora.

But wait, Aurora <u>had</u> said it often happened that matters temporarily got worse for a while, after one started using the new techniques. Looked at from another perspective, moreover, the loss of her job was an opportunity for her to launch into a new and more evolved vocation. Aurora had indeed said each challenge, each setback, should be treated as a golden opportunity, that positive thinking was one of the main keys to change. As for the money, why hadn't she thought of it before, there was always her rich old Uncle Toby. True, he was a totally repulsive toad and the idea of having to lower herself by asking him for a loan wasn't very appealing, but, if she just opened herself to receive, receive she would.

There followed a quick visit to Uncle Toby's. Yes, it seemed he would oblige but in the process of negotiation, Flowing had to submit to a lot of groping and mauling in his little back-room den. She emerged from his house with the cash and most of her dignity intact. She pushed to the back of her mind the revelation that Uncle Toby had just practically raped her. What mattered was that she was beginning to manifest plenty.

Breezily, she announced to Alice and Liz that she would be away for a while, loftily paid up her share of the electricity bill and to demonstrate her plenty, left £30 to pay for any other expenses whilst she was away. Finally, she decided that the best she could do to improve the vibrations of the house in her absence was to buy some flowers. She purchased three magnificent bunches of assorted flowers which she felt transformed the kitchen to a place of beauty. Also, Aurora had instructed her that you always get back what you give out and that by giving, you open yourself to further receipts - a bit of an investment really, Flowing supposed, contemplating the blooms. Alice and Liz looked somewhat bemused by the floral display but thawed enough to wave her goodbye as she set off for her week's exposure to country air.

Her first day at the Creeping Snake Healing Camp was very hectic. It was camping, for a start, and she had omitted to notice on the poster that campers had to bring their own tents. However, wandering round the field the first afternoon feeling a bit lost, she had started chatting to another woman who had come on her own, Maya, and Maya had space in her tent. Maya had also been at a previous camp and knew the ropes. She was in fact staying on all summer. She showed Flowing round the site which consisted of fields, enclosed in hedgerows and within sight of the vista of Glastonbury Hill. It was the energies of the Tor which, Maya told her, had attracted all the campers to

Creeping Snake, powerful healing energies, which would tune them in to working to restore planetary balance.

At first, Flowing felt somewhat doubtful that the grand designs of planetary healing could be effected from such an untogether-looking outfit. Healing groups were to be held in various rather windswept, faded and dilapidated marquees scattered over the site; meals were cooked in an unsanitary-looking caravan and were very overpriced; the hot-tub looked distinctly uninviting with green scum floating on the top; and the toilet facilities consisted of a crude wooden frame which left splinters in the posterior, the frame poised precariously over a distinctly unfragrant-smelling hole - lovingly called the Shit Pit by campers. But she pushed such negative first impressions to the back of her mind, decided to focus on positives, and not be too judgemental. After all, she was a city-kid and things were different in the country.

And, sure enough, after a couple of days roughing it, Flowing began to experience the rigours of the Creeping Snake camp as part of its distinctive charm. She found a way to squat on the toilet seat and avoid lacerations, Maya managed to wheedle big portions of food from friends in the kitchen-crew, and she was so involved in the happenings of the camp, that she was prepared to overlook minor irritations. A crippling bout of dysentery which kept the campers on the trot had given them all the incentive to begin a 36-hour healing-fast. During the workshop on sacred earth energies, a huge thunderstorm broke overhead, most of the marquees leaked badly, but Flowing found that, by going with the energies instead of complaining, wonderful new experiences happened for her. The torrential downpour proved to be an opportunity for the members of the Earth Energies group to throw off their clothes, run out into the rain and experience deep cleansing from the waters of the Earth Mother. Circling around naked, breasts banging against her ribs, Flowing felt wonderfully liberated. This was the first time in her adult life she had been out of doors naked and the rain lashing her skin so furiously awakened powerful sexual feelings in her. She was really beginning to get in touch with her animal self, she thought.

In fact, much of the emphasis of the Creeping Snake camp seemed to be about awakening the Kundalini energy dormant at the base of the spine and many of the most meaningful exchanges during the workshops seemed to culminate in the coming-together of long-lost twin-souls. New couples would disappear into tents for a few hours only to re-appear for subsequent re-unions with freshly discovered souls from their ever-expanding soul-groups. It was all so breathtakingly exciting. Flowing picked up the rudiments of reflexology, learnt about the use of herbs for common ailments, chanted Native American songs by moonlight. She wondered if she too would make a

Karmic connection. With Maya to hang-out with, she wasn't lonely, but being so close to the elements was stirring up much sensual appetite in her, which daily became more pressing.

In a workshop on healing sexual energies, Flowing was instructed in the Tao of Sex. She was to require her male partners to withhold from orgasm as they plied her with thrill after thrill. She discreetly surveyed the men present in the Tao workshop. Would any of these interested seekers want to share such an initiation with her? and which was the most fanciable? Certainly not Rob, veteran hippy gone-to-seed. She hastily averted her eyes from his somewhat too provocatively bold stare. He had been through at least 15 twin-souls in three days. Even if he could keep going all day and all night, she didn't feel turned on by him at all, nor by any of the other men, in fact. Some of the women, however, were stunningly attractive. Strangely, the Healing Sex workshop did not cover the possibilities of unions between women. It concentrated on the sacred marriage of the inner man with the inner woman. Flowing was told by Rod, one of the workshop teachers, that her personal task was to work on being more feminine. He suggested that she open her channels to the Divine Feminine Source by calling upon Her at every opportunity.

This Flowing dutifully did, and things certainly did start to happen. But it was hard to figure out exactly how to work with all the new energies she was invoking. Sitting in the hot-tub one evening by herself, luxuriating in the deep aboriginal heat, she once again called on the Divine Feminine Source. The evening was beautiful, the warmth was soporific, she fell into a drowse. She was dimly aware of another body entering the tub but her eyes were closed. She was concentrating hard on opening herself to be more receptive. She felt power beginning to flood through her, tingling in her spine, a rush of energy to her genitals and breasts. She opened her eyes abruptly. The first thing she saw confronting her shocked eyes was a rather meaty-looking phallus floating on the water directly between her legs. The rather ominous-looking member was attached, she apprehended, to none other than Rob. His long greying hair was hanging like rats' tails round his saucer-like eyes which were, yet again, gazing penetratingly into hers. Panic seized her - did the Divine Feminine Source mean her to open herself to Rob, to allow him to awaken the feminine in her by his masterful strokes? Why else had She thrust this man so close to her in her sacred space? She didn't wait to find out. She made an undignified exit from the hot-tub, the cheeks of her buttocks grazing Rob's left earlobe. He gazed lasciviously after her retreating rear.

Flowing had half decided to bring the matter of etiquette in the hot-tub up at Pow-Wow next morning. Pow-wow was another name for the group-meetings where campers could share their experiences, sort out camp problems, organise happenings for the day and generally experience the magic of getting together together. For Pow-Wows were no ordinary meetings but were solemnly graced by the use of the talking-stick, an idea 'passed on' by Native Americans. Instead of the usual unceremonious style of free-for-all meetings, with the loudest (usually male) voices saying most, the requirement was that people could only speak in turn whilst they had the stick in their hand. This certainly slowed things down a bit and gave the group time to absorb each contribution.

So far, morning Pow-wows had dealt with camp details like dogs raiding tents, a perennial shortage of volunteers for the creche, the rather expensive meals, and changes in workshop-arrangements. Errol, who was the Chief of Creeping Snake ( though, of course, he wasn't really Chief, as the new way of operating was definitely non-hierarchical) presided over the meetings and took unresolved issues back to others in the camp collective. With a beautifully woven Native American rug on his shoulders, holding the feathered stick, Errol had quite a commanding presence. He opened the day's circle with a round of Indian chants. Flowing wondered just how she could bring up her concern for possibly over-intrusive willies in an atmosphere so solemnly sacred and sublime. As it happened, there was an item on the agenda more pressing than Rob's wandering willie. For Errol announced that there had been a serious incident in the camp the night before and that he had decided to bring the matter to PowWow as a matter of urgency.

What seemed to have happened was this. A woman called Rachel had been beaten up by several other campers, and taunted with being a Jew. Rachel and her assailants had met each other before and been involved in a very heavy dispute. This had re-erupted the previous night, and Rachel was, at the end of it all, badly bruised and minus her glasses. Sitting next to Errol, she looked rather shaken. Those who had set upon her, four in number, sat together with an air of confident group-solidarity. The circle was very silent.

Then Errol invited Rachel to speak. She gripped the talking-stick with white knuckles. The story she told was one of a completely out-of-order attack and an unfair one at that, four against one. Moreover, to crown it all, came the anti-semitic abuse. Rachel finished by saying that she had been threatened by the group of four for a couple of days, had alerted Errol, and felt that the time had now come for the four heavies to guarantee no future attack on her or for them to be asked to leave Creeping Snake.

The talking-stick went to the spokeswoman for the Big Four. She stated baldly that Rachel had had it coming to her, and that if she hadn't been such a pathetic wimp, none of it would have happened anyway - a position of unrepentant belligerency, it seemed. Errol seemed not to notice this, or if he did, he let it pass. 'Just let us examine how, as a group, we manifested this heaviness' he intoned. 'And it is also up to the individuals concerned to each take responsibility for creating this situation.' There was a splutter of distress from Rachel. 'What do you mean, Errol?' she demanded. 'Are you saying that I asked to be attacked here?' 'Well, not quite that 'Errol reassured her. 'But you do have to look at your own karma and work out how you attracted this attack, what thoughts you unconsciously have about yourself, what fears you hold, what attitudes you ...' 'I can't take any more' interrupted Rachel, 'are you saying that my attitudes, my fears, created this attack on me? Don't you recognise the phenomenon of anti-Semitism as a real force? Don't you have anti-racist guide-lines at Creeping Snake? Do you think the Jews were responsible for their own genocide?' 'One thing at a time' calmly interposed Errol - 'yes, I think the Jews were ultimately responsible for their own genocide. That is not, of course, to exonerate the Nazis from their role but we have to look at what the Jews were doing that created this karma for them.'

He paused to give time for this pearl of wisdom to sink in. 'For we all have to acknowledge' he finished 'that we are, ultimately, each one of us, one hundred percent responsible for our total reality. A hard lesson, I know, but--- .' 'But' Rachel screamed 'A hard lesson, you say , it's impossible. Not only have I been attacked, but now you're saying that I was one hundred percent responsible for the attack anyway.

24

What next, are you going to suggest that I leave the camp?'

Though her last question was ironical, she looked on the verge of tears. 'Well' Errol said 'in fact, yes, I think it would be best all round if both parties to the dispute were to leave. Creeping Snake isn't really the place for such heavy energies. We have tried to bring resolution to this conflict. And having failed, we want to continue to provide a healing-space for the rest of the camp.' 'Healing?' yelled Rachel. 'What about a safe space for women?!!' 'I can only advise you, in future, Rachel, to surround yourself with thoughts of safety, you will feel safe, and you will be safe' concluded Errol gravely, resting his hand on Rachel's shoulder in a gesture of fatherly kindness. 'I really think we have given enough energy to this dispute. However, has anybody else got any further thoughts on the matter?'

The group was silent for quite some time. The heavy atmosphere had left everyone feeling somewhat shaken-up and confused. What had just happened? Rachel had made a complaint and it had been suggested that she leave. But Errol was an O.K. guy - there must be more going on here than met the eye. The silence continued. A woman eventually mustered herself to say 'I can't say I feel at all happy that Rachel should be asked to leave, Errol.' Errol clutched the talking-stick, drew his blanket wearily round him and said. 'Well, it's all a question of whether we, as individuals or as a group, want to live with victim-consciousness. This attracts really heavy energies to the group. I believe we are at a sort of group-healing crisis. And I feel the best way for it to be resolved is for those involved in the dispute to leave the camp, as I suggested before, and take some space to come to terms with what has happened. When a sore on the body becomes septic, it needs to release the toxins and then it is cleansed and healing commences.' 'What, I am pus now, am I ?' screamed Rachel. She seized her bag, and with a totally white and shocked face, left the Pow-Wow escorted by a friend. The four heavies smirked smugly. 'We'll just have to give the energies time to settle' said Errol, 'let's go on to discuss the arrangements for tonight's sweat-lodge. Who's on the rota for wood-collection?'

The energies around the dispute did seem to settle - Rachel was seen leaving with three of her friends that afternoon and the Big Four stuck it out brazenly for another couple of days - it seemed that the bus they were travelling in was also in a state of healing-crisis and it took some time for it to be repaired. The 'incident', as it came to be described, was discussed by camp-members endlessly, analysed, dissected, looked at from all angles, and then it gradually faded into the background. There was so much else going on, it was hard to stay focussed on that one issue for so long. There were so many other wounds needing to be healed - and they were a whole lot more fun than confronting the gas chambers face-first. And after all, everybody else in the camp seemed to be having such a healing experience. There must be some truth in Errol's position that Rachel had created this experience for herself.

Flowing discussed the healing-crisis at great length with Maya long into the night. They had both got to know and like Rachel over the few days of the Camp and were disconcerted by the turn of events. 'Why,' mused Maya, 'Errol didn't mention persecutor-consciousness at all. I wonder why not?' They also wondered if all the women in the Creeping Snake collective shared Errol's perspective. It seemed that they did and, as they all seemed powerful sussed women, Flowing and Maya felt they should just trust their verdict, novel though their ideas on social justice might be.

And as it happened, Flowing soon didn't have much space for rational thought. She finally let the healing energies of Creeping Snake get in to her and opened herself to a powerful change of consciousness. It had happened like this. Maya and Flowing used to wash their undies by hand and hang them on a hawthorn hedge to dry. The morning after Creeping Snake's healing crisis, Flowing had in vain searched for her knickers. She even pushed her way through the hedge into the next field to ferret around the undergrowth there on the chance that the wind had blown them over. But there was no sign of the missing garments. Slightly dishevelled and distraught, Flowing propped herself against a nearby pine-tree to take stock of things.

It was a beautiful fresh morning, the sun was rising, she could smell breakfasts cooking nearby. She felt a sensation of communion with all beings creeping over her. And then she heard a rustle beside her. Crouching in the long grass nearby was a stunningly handsome man, with long dark hair braided a la Sioux style, which he carried with a natural poise. Errol could learn a thing or two from him on authenticity, Flowing noted. He had softly hypnotic brown eyes and was smiling at her through the grass. There was a long silence. Flowing felt she should say something to explain her presence, but what? 'I was just looking for something' she eventually managed to come up with. 'Was it these?' he asked, holding up her knickers in a strong bronzed hand. 'Well, no' Flowing lied, flooded with embarrassment at the sight of her undies in the intimate clutch of a male stranger. 'Just our dishcloth. Must have got blown away' she burbled. 'Yes?' he said, and rose towards her. 'Shall I help you back through the hedge? It's a bit thick here.'

She felt his warm firm muscles as she pushed past him through the foliage and detected a delectable male odour. He asked her name. 'I'm Leaning Pine' he added. 'Leaning Pine?' she repeated. She had been leaning on a pine when she first glimpsed him and moreover it was a leaning pine. This must be what the Creeping Snakers meant by synchronicity, she thought, things happening together, a sign she was beginning to get into the flow. 'Would you like to see my bender?' Leaning Pine asked her, guiding her to a little hut built of tarpaulin draped over bent saplings. She crawled after him into the entrance. The interior was dark, warm, and womb-like, but, as her eyes grew accustomed to it, she gasped in astonishment. All around her were sacred Indian artefacts, rugs, pipes, feather head-dresses - she suddenly felt herself transported to another time and place, one where folk lived simply in touch with the earth energies. On the floor were thick sheepskin rugs which looked freshly slept in.

Flowing found herself sinking onto them and Leaning Pine slowly bending down over her. Silently they came together. It quickly became apparent that Leaning Pine hadn't attended the workshop on the Tao of Sex - he exploded forcefully inside her almost instantaneously. Such was Flowing's pent-up desire and her sense of connection with him, and with everything in fact, that she came too, in a flood of passion that totally unnerved her. She found herself trembling naked in the arms of a total stranger.

But he proved to be very nice - he called her 'little sister.' He had a wide slow smile, and, in the moments before their next communion, he shared a little of himself with her. He was part of the Creeping Snake crew, this was his third summer at the camps, during winter he lived in a Tepee Circle in a remote valley in

Scotland. It seemed, Flowing thrilled to hear, that he was 'between relationships', his ex having left him some weeks previously to explore new spaces. How she could have left such a miracle as Leaning Pine, Flowing couldn't imagine. But as she had a toddler daughter, it may have been something to do with the fact that she had found life in a bender too constricting, cosy enough as a couple's love-nest though it might be.

In the last couple of days of the Healing Camp, she spent much time in the confines of Leaning Pines' bender. By final Pow-wow and the last night's celebration party, Flowing felt herself unable to part from him, and he from her. With a stroke of luck, or more accurately, Flowing noted, with the energies working for them, a vacancy came up in the camp-site office-crew and Leaning Pine managed to swing it for her. Flowing found herself a member of the Creeping Snake collective and looked forward to a long and growthful summer.

# CHAPTER 3
## A TRIP UP THE LEFT-HAND PATH?

And the summer proved an adventure for Flowing. Every day, through the varied fabric of Sacred Dance week, Astrology week, a week on American Indian lore, and yet more --- she felt herself drinking in more and more of the sacred, becoming more and more in touch with the healing forces of nature, and in particular with the healing force of the touch of Leaning Pine. Life was a constant whirl, from the first stirrings of camp life at dawn to the moment of shut-eye, encircled in Leaning Pine's strong arms and lulled to sleep by rhythmic drumming and chanting from the near-by camp-fire. She spent several hours a day at the Group Rhythms Co-ordination tent earning her keep, snatched as many sessions as she could at whatever workshop was happening in her free time and finished the day with a couple of hours of' sensual massage on the sheepskins with Leaning Pine.

Over the course of the weeks, she picked up the Creeping Snakes' knowledge of the sacred American Indian path as transmitted by Thundering Whelk, a Cherokee medicine-man who had been guided by a vision to share his teachings with white folk. He attended the camp for one week with several members of his tribe and the whole time of his stay was the highlight of the Creeping Snake summer. Here were real live Indians with a real live religion and a precious opportunity to be guided back into the old ways, the ways that had served humans for millennia, the ways that had ensured balance and harmony between all beings.

Flowing let her hair grow long, sometimes plaited it in braids and twined it with feathers. Thundering Whelk trained camp members to attend to the flights of birds, the rustling of trees, the movement of creeping beings through the grasses. Most of all he was into Healing. He carried a crystal, animal hooves, bird feathers, rocks and told his students about the Medicine Wheel. His visit culminated in a magnificent Sweat Lodge ceremony. Flowing managed to avoid the still importunate Rob in the moist, muddy dark recesses of the Lodge and guided by Thundering Whelk's sonorous voice muttering strange incantations, purified by sage smoke, she distinctly felt an awakening of contact with the Ancestors. All in all, something real and big was happening to her. Ensconced in Creeping Snake camp all through the summer weeks, she barely thought of her past life and friends or her future direction - keeping in the here and now took all her energy.

But as the closing days of the Creeping Snake summer-cycle neared, Flowing had to ponder her next move. What should she do next? She had had a wonderful summer. But winter was clearly on its way, there had been ice on the water that morning. And all good things had to come to an end. Perhaps she should go back home and apply her new awareness to city-life. She shuddered at the very thought of being cramped in city streets after the freedom of the fields. She doubted whether she could glimpse many feathered friends, hear many hoofed beings, or be startled by any pavement sightings of creeping cousins in her urban habitat. Her hopes of continuing her communion with all beings were battling hard with the tests of twenty first-century reality and despair began to set in. Perhaps she should forget it all and sign up for a course on web-site design.

But then, whilst she was mentally choosing the colour of her new I-Pad, words of Aurora's came back to her. She had said that all good things needn't come to an end, that that was part of the limiting bunk that she must jettison. Life was a never-ending round of joy and abundance. Of course, the love, warmth and learning of the summer could continue. She tentatively opened up the matter of the future with Leaning Pine late one night after a particularly long and fervent lovemaking. But Flowing got a nasty jolt. Leaning Pine seemed to stiffen at the words 'future, commitments, making it together through life's bye-ways'. As Flowing got deeper into the subject, he distinctly bridled, became positively cool. It seemed his path was one of remaining open to the flow, to whatever life threw up, including whatever new spiritual possibilities might come his way to evolve all sorts of new meaningful relationships.

The conversation foundered in total impasse with Flowing feeling submerged in woe. Leaning Pine tried to tell her it was all cool, she could hang out with him over the winter, but she would have to understand that there might be other ladies on the sheepskin rugs - not a prospect Flowing found easy to stay cool about. Leaning Pine gently assured her that the way forward was to let go of old patterns of possessiveness, that jealousy came from feelings of limitation and fears that there was not enough love in the universe. Sure enough, Flowing remembered the very same words from Aurora. Aurora had confided that several times in her former past, she had been at the mercy of jealousy. This was until she realised that being in love was merely a state of being, of being in love with the universe, with life itself and ultimately with one's own self. From that point on, she had flowed smoothly through the years in a flood of love, warmth and bliss, all jealous pangs a thing of the past.

But could Flowing make such a massive breakthrough? At the moment, she was sorely tempted to take a vengeful bite out of Leaning Pine's comforting shoulder. She felt like she was being carried on the back of a fierce charger over which she had not the slightest control and that at any moment, she might go wildly on the rampage through Creeping

Snake camp, shattering the silent night with howls of rage and hurt. The carefully cultivated high vibrations of the camp healing-circle would be utterly destroyed by such a ruckus. That would not be on. She grabbed a few belongings and dashed sobbing over the grass to Maya's tent.

By co-incidence, Maya was very much in the same space. She had gotten close to Errol over the last few days, a real big deal, seeing as he was the Chief (well, not really) of the whole Creeping Snake venture. Getting between his sheets (or more accurately onto his bracing buffalo-hide bed) had opened up several doors for her - he had suggested she stay on over the winter at Creeping Snake headquarters as part of the team organising next summer's work, earning some money, and celebrating festivals together. It had all sounded highly attractive. But, as the conversation progressed, Maya began not to like the lie of the land. Errol's vision was one of Maya fitting into a team which consisted of him and several women, all of whom, it seemed, were into him and, it seemed, thrived on it. Maya had felt sick-at-heart.

'What are we going to do?' they moaned simultaneously, crying then laughing together. 'Shit, we're in a mess' Flowing sighed. 'Perhaps we should do some work on possessiveness, really try to get a handle on it. I mean I couldn't ever go through all this again.' 'Nope, nor me' assented Maya. 'But what are we going to do, and where?' They were both at a loss.

But, remembering recent lessons, they both affirmed that life, from its abundance, would come up with an answer and sure enough, next morning, it did.

Maya was brushing her teeth at the camp-pump, chatting to a new woman, Shakti, about their dilemmas. Shakti, suddenly very excited, said she knew of the very thing for them. Then a doubtful look crossed her brow. 'Hm, I'm not sure if this workshop is open for non-sannyasins but I'll see if I can get you on, if you are interested. It's all about opening to divine love through the Tantric path and it is an experiential group - no head-trips allowed, all heavy body-work and meditation to get through blocks. Interested?' 'Well yes,' said Maya,' certainly we need some powerful therapy. But what are sannyasins?' Shakti briefly filled her in. She was a follower of an enlightened Master, Whambam. Round her neck she had a mala, a bead necklace from which a snapshot of Whambam's face beamed out significantly. He was a Tantric guru from the East who had decided to share its sex-mysteries with the West, at cut-price. His followers run workshops at their centres throughout the world. And there was to be one the very next weekend in London. They should get back to her by the end of the day and let her know whether they had decided this was for them.

Maya and Flowing thought long and hard about the prospect of a weekend's gruelling therapy. Money didn't need to be an obstacle as Maya had quite a sum from a legacy and could pay for Flowing's weekend. Flowing gulped gratefully. But she did have initial misgivings over being part of a group taking orders, albeit spiritual ones, from a man. On the other hand, only recently, she had been advised to open herself to the Feminine, to be more receptive. Perhaps this path would encourage her to go the whole hog, not just be any old doormat, even a spiritual one, but to lay aside her rebellious daughter of the patriarchy trip once and for all. The spirit of surrender to Whambam might be just the lesson she needed. For he was no ordinary guru, he was a sex guru, and in sex, a woman was at her most receptive and open to the male. Really, given the emotional mess she was in, did she have anything to lose? At least Whambam offered her the chance of releasing these violently heavy feelings, moving her love for Leaning Pine onto a different and higher level, far removed from petty jealousies over mine and thine.

So by the end of the day, they said yes to Shakti who had, in fact, managed to secure places for them on the workshop. From then on, time passed quickly, until the final day of the Creeping Snake summer camps arrived. Flowing and Maya said farewell to all, both trying and succeeding in looking cool about goodbyes to their respective men, whilst both in the grip of devouring grief. Flowing cast one last look at Leaning Pine, standing as poised and beautiful as ever by the gate, waving goodbye to them as they drove off down the lane. She smiled breezily back and once safely round a bend, let out half an hour's strangulated sobs. Maya was in a bit of a better state having been involved with Errol for less time. They comforted each other with the thought that, if they managed to work through their stuff, they would soon be able to cope with the idea of a re-union with their loves in a spirit of sharing, co-operation and harmony. Flowing, however, was left with a dull ache in her heart.

Pre-occupied with their feelings as they were on their exit from the camp, they both failed to register a tight knot of strangers gathered near the gate, bearing placards. Flowing briefly caught a flash of words. 'Hands off Native American religion. No to plastic medicine-men. Thundering Whelk is a fraud'. She heard a chant very different in pitch and content from those of the last few weeks - angrily yelled, it said:

*'You can't sell the Spirit, She is like a mountain*
*Old and strong, she goes on and on.'*

But concentrating on blotting out her own emotions as she was, she succeeded also in blotting out this.

# CHAPTER 4

# TANTRIC MYSTERIES REVEALED

From the first moment of the workshop, things were ultra-heavy indeed. The event was mainly for initiated sannyasins who had worked on heavy shit before and Flowing and Maya had gotten themselves in at the deep end. However, the workshop leader, a slim bearded man in his early forties by the name of Bhigwhata ( or was it Whatabiga or Whatabuga? ) was gentle on them and spent a few minutes easing them into things. 'What's happening now' he said, motioning to the room full of gyrating, screaming and kicking sannyasins, 'is that we're letting it all out, a catharsis of all the frustrations, hurts and tensions. We find the music gives it more energy.' A tape was pounding out a rhythmical electrical beat which built up to periodic crescendos, accompanied by crescendos of curses, yells, hair-tearing by the hordes of sannyasins. All clad in skimpy red tunics, they looked a force to be reckoned with. Was this what love was all about? thought Flowing. It was certainly a power capable of conquering all. It was petrifying. Wave after wave of violent emotional anguish swept the room.

'Best thing to do is to go straight with it' murmured Bhigwhata, pushing them both firmly into the yelling mob. He turned up the music. It assaulted the ears, its pulsating speed accompanied by flashing lights. The pressure to belong to the throng was irresistible. Maya and Flowing found themselves joining the herd, ripping through their defences, carefully constructed through years of repressive childhoods, defying social conventions, and acting outright crazy. Maya tore her garments to shreds, shrieked like a banshee, and rolled on the floor. Flowing had her first full-throated tantrum since the age of three, lying flat on her back, pumping legs all around her, and pumped her own legs back and forth on the floor, yelling 'No No No' at the top of her voice. 'Yes Yes Yes' screamed a red-faced man, Bhigwata's assistant, his eyes bulging as he egged her on. 'No No No' she defied him. 'Yes Yes Yes' he thundered. The energy release was terrific.

But this, it seemed, was only the beginning. Bhigwata let the dishevelled, sweating and semi-exhausted group rest for a few minutes. 'Now' he said, 'we've got to begin working on releasing rage and hurt felt towards the opposite sex. I want men up at this end of the room and you women down at the other. When I shout "Get primitive", I want you to get primitive. No holds barred. The only rule is "Stop. I mean it." If things get beyond the point you're comfortable with, yell "Stop I mean it." That's the rule. Do you all understand?' It seemed they all did. Bhigwhata turned on another tape. It was an amplified and speedy heartbeat which reverberated through the furthest recesses of the brain. 'Get primitive' he yelled. And obediently, they did.

Lined up with all the women at one end of the room, Flowing and Maya charged with their sisters towards the other end, where, luckily for them, a smaller number of men were preparing for battle. They lunged at each other, fists flying, swirling cushions or rubber batons, ripping clothes, pummelling shoulders, lunging at balls, mouthing the most odious expletives they could muster. Bhigwhata looked on with benign approval. One enterprising woman seized a lamp- stand and staggering across the room with it, landed it fair and square on the head of a particularly infuriating-looking male. Bhigwhata, looking slightly pained at the damage done to the lamp-stand, removed the broken fragments rather pointedly. The infuriating-looking male lay spread-eagled prostrate on the floor. He looked radiantly happy. Far from shouting 'Stop I mean it' he seemed to be begging for more. Flowing really let him have it.

She hadn't dreamt she had it in her. A well of rage seized her and she punched the podgy figure for all her worth, yelling 'You pig, you bloody pig, I detest you. You abomination.' He absorbed it all like putty, and Flowing reared to her feet to find some other male with a bit more fight. Ultimately, she didn't get a kick out of the male-jelly getting a kick out of her getting a kick at him. She zoned in on another male whose long black locks reminded her of Leaning Pine. 'You bastard, you bastard' she growled, seizing him by the neck and aiming for his balls with her feet. He fought back and pretty soon they were rolling on the floor, with him eventually getting the upper hand. 'Sisters, sisters' shrieked Flowing. Three women came to her support and grabbed the Leaning Pine look-alike from her like a rag doll and tossed him into a corner. He got to his feet, looking even more ready for battle. With two male allies, he squared with Flowing's mob and bodies locked in a sweating mass, reminiscent to Flowing of past oafish sexual encounters. The tide of rage within her and the other women grew to frenzy stage. As one body, they suddenly acted in concert, rounded up all the men, dumped them on a heap of cushions in the centre of the room, and circled round them in a war-dance complete with war-cry. As they pounded round and round their prisoners, the held-back rage of their mothers and foremothers, silenced by centuries of male oppression, brought their blood to the boil. In their very bones, they knew it was time for sweet revenge.

'Stop!' thundered Bhigwhata. He deftly flicked a switch on the music-tape. 'Time to change the energy, from release through catharsis, to release through celebration. Dance! Dance! and remember, there is only the dance.' Wispy Indian music filled the sound system. A few men staggered to their feet and began loping around to the dance-music. The women were a bit thrown at first by the sudden let-down of their climax. But it seemed they were used to this sort of thing and they all, within seconds, threw themselves into the dance. And by the end of the tape, sure enough, they were all feeling tremendously high. True, there were a few black eyes, bruises and possibly a broken arm. But they had got rid of so much shit and experienced the genuine liberation from crippling social mores that only followers of Whambam could experience to the limit. Sure, there were bound to be casualties. But they were now getting ready to get down to the real business of the workshop this afternoon - coupling in the Tantric embrace.

How was the leap to be made from the wild aggro of the morning to the controlled meditative copulative high of Tantric union? Flowing and Maya pondered over lunch, looking forward to finding out. At the same time, they were both undeniably anxious about how the coupling was to come about. There were quite a few particularly unsavoury-looking prospective partners about and they wondered which women would be unfortunate enough to be attempting ecstasy with them. The thought crossed both their minds that many of the men attending the workshop didn't have a hope of attracting a second glance outside of this set-up, let alone of conquering a woman pioneer of sexual peaks. Neither of them, however, gave utterance to such a sentiment.

As it turned out, Bhigwhata next called the group together for a preliminary discussion of the practices of Tantra. The sexual act was to focus on eye-contact, the man had to withhold from orgasm, and both partners had to bring their energy from the genitals to the crown chakra, thus refining it from its crude physical expression. The sacred rite (or Maithuna as it was called) could be performed by two women, and the combination of the two yin energies represented Tantra at an advanced level. It seemed that the union of two men, however, was frowned upon - the two yang energies combined went into reverse and sent the Kundalini energy all haywire. 'Bad news for gays' thought Flowing.

It seemed Bhigwhata almost read her mind. 'Now one word here. Things aren't what they used to be and in these times, we have to be aware of the risk of AIDS and other infections. Moreover, some of you ladies might not be using contraceptives. For these reasons, I want all men to keep one sock on at all times and inside your sock I want you to keep a supply of condoms. Ladies, you are to carry rubber gloves for yourselves and your prospective partners in little belts around the waist. I want you to regard these necessary protectives' - he motioned to a table laden with little packages - 'as spiritual tools and to try to get into their sexual possibilities.'

Flowing's mind, already reeling, almost lurched into non-functioning at the prospect of transforming rubber gloves into spiritual tools. But more was to come. 'For the advanced ladies of Sappho's school, there are the dental dams' and he motioned to some contraptions which more resembled mediaeval torture-devices than instruments of pleasure. Bhigwhata seemed to register her distress for, at this point, he continued 'You'll find that the accessories won't get in the way at all, not once the energy is moving. Next, I want you to get into pairs, any combination except man with man, of course, and sit in the meditation-position opposite each other, maintaining eye-contact all through. I want you to visualise your partner as an expression of the blossoming of divinity, look beyond the purely personal level. You are to change partners every fifteen minutes.' 'What?' thought Flowing, 'Every fifteen minutes - hope he doesn't follow this schedule for the sexual coupling.' Moreover the task of seeing some of the assorted male specimens before her eyes as blossoms of divinity was a bit of a tall order.

As it turned out, she got a lot out of the eye-to eye meditation. As she focussed on each different face, strange changes went over the features, sometimes she saw a wise old being, sometimes a shy maiden, sometimes a Persian overlord, it was a glimpse into a different dimension. The music had been switched off and for the first time in many days, she felt a sort of peace. If only she could keep in this space.

'Now' broke in Bhigwhata 'keep in this meditative space, calm and peaceful. Over on the table here I have some blindfolds. Quietly put them on, then I want you to remove your clothes, and start exploring the room and the bodies you meet in it. Your eyes are blind-fold to cut out visual prejudice. I want you to respond purely body-to-body, to get in touch with your sexual energy at its basic level. I suggest that you crawl around the floor and get into your animal selves. Make noises if it helps. What we are doing in this session is becoming aware of the responses of the physical body to different physical bodies. In this process, find the body or bodies you feel most attuned to, the one you will later on be working with to bring the mutual enjoyment to a culmination and refining it for spiritual advancement. At this stage, let anything happen short of intercourse. Be bold.' 'My god' thought Flowing 'what will my body come up with?' She quickly closed her eyes to expunge the vision of the overlarge man she had been previously kicking to bits. Looking distinctly walrus-like, he was gazing at her longingly. 'What if I don't get turned on at all?' voiced another woman. 'Trust the body' soothed Bhigwhata. 'If it's meant to happen, it will happen.'

He flicked the light-switch and the room was plunged into semi-darkness. 'Get your blindfolds' he commanded and turned on a tape that oozed saxophonic sensuality. The group covered their eyes dutifully and fell onto their knees - they began tentatively crawling about. The bolder members commenced nuzzling at each other. Flowing shambled about, heading to what she hoped would be the safety of a corner, where she could muster some more nerve. But as she went, she came alongside another crawling body, big and warm. It reached out an arm and embraced her round the waist. It felt O.K. She extended her hand and engaged with a strong muscular chest. She heard the stranger's breathing speed up and her own did. She stroked further and felt a definite masculinity. It reared up to greet her. Should she go on? She did and once the ice was broken, she moved on to greet another body. This one proved a bit of a disappointment. She puzzled as to how to disengage from the embryonic embrace without hurting any feelings. In the end, she decided ' So what? He can't see whose discarding him - time to move on' and she shoved him firmly off and crawled onward. She explored several bodies, none quite so inviting as her first encounter, and none so dynamically thrilling as the touch of Leaning Pine's little finger.

However, she was opening herself up now. And Leaning Pine wasn't one hundred percent on her mind, one hundred percent of the time. She had much more urgently pressing matters to hand, like the astoundingly large penis she had just brushed by. Was it real? She did not have a chance to find out as she discovered another woman had got there first. So she moved on to delicately explore several women's bodies and greatly enjoyed it. Things were getting interesting.

She wondered if any of the women she had caressed could have been Maya. One woman seemed to have her distinctive tousled curls. The music was slowing down and Bhigwhata started to speak again. 'Now slowly' he said 'I want you to take off your blindfolds. Look about you and move towards those you feel attracted to. Keep in touch, however, with your body-responses. Throw off any inhibitions and let go and enjoy yourself to the uttermost. There are masses of cushions around. And don't forget your protectives. I'll be keeping an eye on things just in case.'

'This is it' thought Flowing 'can I go through with this?' As she strapped on her belt of protective rubber gloves, her eyes met Maya's. She looked similarly dubious. They both speculatively eyed the display of male bodies, now naked, not much of a choice. Flowing had her eye on her Leaning Pine look-alike. But it seemed several others also had. For, when Bhigwhata gave the order, she found herself in an undignified melee around him. 'Heck, too much competition' she thought, and turning away, she banged into a reasonably attractive older man who opened his arms to her. She fell into them, if only as it relieved her of any further open-eyed group embarrassment. They kissed and started to get to know each other's bodies. She didn't remember him from the first blind encounters. What next? She could hear the beginning sounds of uninhibited sexual performances around her and noticed several couples already at it, writhing on the floor. She wondered how they had managed to kit themselves up in rubber so speedily.

But she had little time for further speculation as her male partner was whispering in her ear, suggesting she prepare them for action. The time had come for a decision. Flowing decided. True, this man was a total stranger, he might be married with several kids, he might be a homicidal maniac, but she had got this far, she couldn't turn back now. She threw herself into the ensuing orgy, gloves and all and the next couple of hours passed in a welter of heaving bodies, rolling bestially on the floor.

The proceedings were drawn to a close by Bhigwhata once again. He called the group to him and they sat in rows at his feet, hair matted with sweat and the air pungent with the fragrance of many bodies. Bhigwhata's female assistant deftly removed the litter of rubber debris from the floor. 'Now to move the energy up to the heart chakra,' intoned Bhigwhata. They passed the next hour chanting 'Ah' and focussing on the third eye, memories of the previous session's lower chakra activities slowly subsiding. Besides, they were now feeling somewhat spent. Flowing became aware that the dull ache in her heart, first experienced on her departure from Leaning Pine, was still there. But tomorrow heart-energy was to be moved up to the crown chakra and transmuted. There was still hope.

Next morning, Bhigwhata outlined the plan for the

day. They were to forego breakfast, spend two hours meditating on the crown chakra and then purify themselves for the Maithuna by a ritual bath, followed by a ritual feast. Sounds alright, mused Flowing, who was still, however, non-plused as to how the unseemly orgy of the day before was to be transmuted into a transformative ecstatic experience that would electrically raise the vibrations of all the atoms of her being. And the morning did pass quietly and smoothly to the background lulling of Eastern pipes and the scent of sandalwood incense. They ritually bathed themselves in waters strewn with rosepetals, they ritually feasted on oysters in mushroom and ambergris sauce, followed by delicately spiced halva - all foods noted as aphrodisiacs.

The time came for the Grand Rite. Bhigwhata told them solemnly of the need for Tantric initiates to face the death of the lower self. He described the many long nights spent by Indian seekers sleeping in graveyards to acquaint themselves with the energy of death. However, he assured them, Whambam had set up structures for Westerners to move into the magic of Maithuna swiftly, without the rigours of having to pay their reverences to rigor mortis. This weekend would set them well on their way.

The room was prepared by the group for the Grand Rite. Black candles were lit, more powerful incense readied. The time had come. Bhigwhata struck a huge gong. 'Move in silence to where the energy feels strongest for you' he instructed 'and then get into a meditative posture. As numbers are odd, some women will be paired together, those ready to work at such an advanced level.' An uneasy self-conscious shuffling of bodies followed. Flowing found herself propelled swiftly towards her Leaning Pine look-alike. His popularity had declined dramatically since the previous day's mad scramble towards him. Did he have some acute sexual problem? worried Flowing. But he did seem keen on her. And next thing she knew, she found herself seated comfortably on a cushion contemplating his naked body, which was already slightly beaded with sweat.

The room took some time to settle as the would-be Tantric travellers made the crucial choice of partners. 'Now' Bhigwhata continued, 'the energies of Maithuna are so powerful and require such a level of trust and safety that normally the rite is solemnised through a marriage contract, usually for a year, renewable, or for a lifetime. Through the special procedures designed for the maturer climate of the West, we have created a climate of deep group-safety. Our sacred marriage is, as all you devotees know, to that most advanced of beings, to Whambam, so let us focus on this together to re-consecrate our vows.'

At this, Flowing felt distinctly uneasy. She herself wasn't a sannyasin and moreover she wondered about the ethics of the marriage of the men to Whambam. Hadn't they been told earlier on that the union of two yang energies sent the Kundalini into a negative spiral. But her partner was smiling transfixingly at her and all her reservations flew out of the window. She had no time to contemplate her doubts when she was any second now about to enter into deep sexual union with this attractive stranger. 'Meditate on each other's third eye' rumbled Bhigwhata from somewhere very far away. 'And when the time is right, move into the Tantric position, remembering to maintain eye-contact.' 'And remembering your protectives' he hastened to add.

Flowing focussed on her partner's eyes. They were soft, brown and beautiful. He reached towards her. But as he did so, the mala round his neck struck her on the cheek. Her eyes were drawn to the face of Whambam emblazoned on its centre. The features suddenly seemed rather sleazy, almost drugged with debauchery. She returned her gaze hurriedly to the more wholesome features of her partner. He smiled slowly at her and as he did so, his resemblance to Leaning Pine increased. And the pain in her heart, which had been dormant for a few hours, suddenly assumed the stranglehold of a tourniquet. Surely there was one vital ingredient missing in the impending spiritual exercise? Could it be love? Admittedly the Whambamers felt that their love for their Master brought them all together into a love-space. But wasn't it easier to love a remote stranger deified as perfect rather than the visibly flawed creations that humans inevitably were? She suddenly knew she couldn't go on. She scrambled to her feet, ran to the corner where her clothes lay, and without a backward glance at the intensely preoccupied couples, she attempted to leave the room.

However, Bhigwhata blocked the way. 'Having a problem, Flowing ?' he asked. 'Yes' she blurted 'I don't love him.' 'You don't feel love for your partner?' Bhigwhata repeated. He seemed puzzled. The problem seemed a novel one to him. 'I do find your response strange, Flowing. We have found it is women who are most drawn to the sexual and spiritual liberation of Whambam's path. But then' he continued 'I know that your sentiments have in the past been expressed by those unfortunates who have not experienced the love-energy of the sacred Master. Or' he reflected 'perhaps the problem is that the left-hand path is not the path for you.'

'The left-hand path?' gasped Flowing, intrigued. 'Yes' explained Bhigwhata. He waxed lyrical. 'The initiate on the left-hand path works to enlightenment through engaging to the full in the physical world of the senses, seeing each blossom, each fragrant dish, each lover as a gift from the Divine to be accepted, to be enjoyed and to promote higher consciousness.' He paused, motioning round the room to illustrate his point. 'The right -hand path, by contrast, goes for the ascetic approach, and brings the seeker to truth through denial of gratification.' 'Isn't there anything in between?' Flowing asked. It was a bit of a stark choice, the fleshpots or the hair-shirt. Certainly, she had already experienced more than enough of the former this weekend to last her several lifetimes and she hadn't found it particularly uplifting to her spirits. 'Well, there are as many paths, I suppose, as there are travellers,' conceded Bhigwhata. 'But, Flowing, I feel you should really try to return to the group and work your way through the blocks you are facing.'

Flowing took one last glance around the room. The couples seemed to be blissfully at it in solemn silence. She noticed that her abandoned partner had somehow inveigled himself into a threesome with two women. 'No thanks' she retorted. 'If my road is so blocked, I'm turning back to find another way through.' And she rushed out of the door, swinging it forcefully in the face of the somewhat disconcerted Bhigwhata.

It was several hours before Flowing and Maya met up again. Flowing had gone for a long walk through the streets to fill in the time and had conducted a thorough post-mortem on her brush with the path of ecstasy. It had thrown her somewhat to hear Bhigwhata say that women were very attracted to the Way of Whambam, for it did seem that there were more women than men on the Whambam path. Was there something wrong with her that she couldn't let go at the Maithuna? Was she afraid of bliss, or still suffering from an infantile projection onto one partner when she could be enjoying the plenty that the

Whambam left-hand path promised. Perhaps she was just afraid that she might get as hooked on her Maithuna-mate as she had been on Leaning Pine. In which case, her possessiveness-problem hadn't budged one inch, in spite of all the work she'd put in that weekend, sharing bodies as liberally as the mind could fantasise. But, her mind continued, who could possibly mind sharing something or somebody they weren't really attached to anyway? The original problem was the pronounced force of her attachment to Leaning Pine. And she hadn't really tested that one out, hadn't had to share him with a horde of eager rivals. All in all, she had learnt one thing this weekend, this particular variant of the left-hand path wasn't the way for her. But what about Maya?

Maya emerged from the work-shop in a state of numb silence. At first, it was hard for Flowing to elicit from her details of her attempt at total transformation. Bit by bit, however, Flowing got the gradual drift of what had transpired. Maya had embarked on the joint belly-breathing when all hell had let loose in the room. It seemed that one woman near Maya had been in the process of eagerly embracing her partner when her eye fell on Maya's man, with whom, it turned out, she had celebrated her last Maithuna. Overtaken by an access of primal feelings, presumably not adequately vented in the previous day's free-for-all, she flounced over to Maya, cast her rudely aside and set upon her partner with full force.

This seemed to trigger massive reactions in those around her and bedlam ensued. In the course of the fray, the 'Stop I mean it' rule seemed to be temporarily suspended. Several sannysins started lashing themselves with their malas, which, being made of tough fibreglass, created quite a sensation. Others regressed to infantile toilet-training hang-ups and got into re-experiencing the delights of faecal play. And finally, three men, evidently straight but needing to act out protest against the prohibitions of a father-figure, cornered Bhigwhata and, on pains of heavy-duty overload of the Kundalini, proceeded to rape him.

All in all, it took about an hour for the room to return to calm, if the state of quiescent exhausted shock could be termed calm. Bhigwhata, looking extremely the worse for wear, assembled himself somewhat shakily after his testing experience. Gathering together his torn garments, he began falteringly to pull his flock together. 'Well' he managed to stammer 'ordeals abound for those on the path of ecstasy - but' recovering his purpose manfully he added 'As Whambam says, there is only the dance - and the dance goes on.'

At this cue, the sannyasins staggered into the centre of the room, slumped into a circle and began to chant in Indian, at first rather dejectedly, but rallying as the minutes passed. They nursed each other's bruises, and began to gaze meaningfully into each other's eyes. Maya had been standing to one side throughout and was by now wondering what it was all about. At this point, the chanting conveniently broke into English. 'It'll all come clear, in the end, It'll all come clear.' Finally, the group managed to hurl itself body-and-soul into a dance celebrating the finale of the Initiation into Tantra workshop (Part III). Maya left them excitedly discussing arrangements for their next bash at the Maithuna. She could only surmise that they were all completely addicted to a powerful fix of ritual ordeals, followed by ritual comfortings, followed by ritual flights into celebration, the whole shaky edifice cemented together by limitless sexual opportunity. Whatever her blocks might be, Part IV of the Tantra Workshops was not her way forward. There must be an easier path to enlightenment.

Flowing was almost as stunned by Maya's account of proceedings as Maya had been in the experiencing of them. They lent limply against the gatepost of the Sannyas Centre, quite at a loss as to what to do next. It was at this point that they were both more than ready for the right-hand path.

# CHAPTER 5

# RIGHT-ON? ON THE RIGHT-HAND PATH

'Had a distressing weekend?' asked a rather wholesome-looking mature woman in a wholesome-looking outfit of lambs-wool twin-set, plaid skirt and stout Birkenstock sandals. She had been standing watching Flowing and Maya for the last few minutes as they slowly tried to get themselves together to leave the Sannyas Centre. 'Yes' they simultaneously exhaled. 'They specialise in traumatic weekends, my dears' said the soundly-sensible voice of their rescuer, who appeared more and more like an unlikely cross between a genial upper-class matron and a knowing crone. Her name was Ethel. 'Perhaps you could do with a chat and a cup of tea. I happen to live nearby and have had quite a lot of experience of salvaging some of the wreckage. Come with me.' Relieved of the burden of deciding what to do next, Flowing and Maya trooped after Ethel.

Her little flat was a haven of peace and domesticity after the excruciating emotional extravaganza of the Sannyas Centre. Two cats lay dozing innocently by the stove, crystals sparkled delicately in the evening sunlight, and there was no suggestion at all in the air of the heavy compulsive sensuality of their previous scene. On the contrary, the decor in Ethel's flat suggested a tempered refined approach to all of the senses. Vivaldi was playing quietly in the background and soon a comforting cup of Quiet Time Herbal tea was readied. Maya and Flowing unburdened their souls of the traumas of the last few hours. Ethel looked grave and thoughtful, nodding her head knowingly at times.

'Sounds to me as if you both have had quite enough of heaviness for quite some time, wouldn't you agree' she twinkled. 'Time for some light energy, wouldn't you say?' 'Too true' they both assented. 'And for some real love-energy too' added Flowing, bitterly re-experiencing for a moment the romantic let-downs of the last few weeks. 'Well, I know just the place for both of you, a place to go and recharge your spiritual batteries and return refreshed to your spiritual paths. Have you heard of Ginborn, Centre for Limitless Light and Love?'

Neither of them had, so Ethel filled them in. Built near a sacred power-point in the wilds of Scotland, the Ginborn community was the centre of a network of world-servers, all dedicated to ushering in the New Age and all working hard on the inner to bring it into being. As part of their work, they had built various centres in many parts of the world consecrated to grounding Aquarian energies. They were open to those seriously committed to planetary service and ran introductory weeks, fortnights or months. Ethel described her life as a member of Ginborn for seven years as one of increasing attunement to her own spiritual being. She had left to bring the Light to a new centre in London. She urged them both to give Ginborn a try.

They needed no urging. Anything that could be an antidote to their recent self-centred excesses was in order and a dose of planetary service could, they thought to themselves rather shame-facedly, put an end to their preoccupation with the Self and its enlightenment. With the earth toiling under loads of noxious toxins, was this the time for them to be toiling after cosmic orgasms? Surely not. They embarked straight-away next morning on the journey north to Scotland and the Ginborn community. Maya's money, it seemed, was still plentifully available and the £585 per week fee for a week at Ginborn was now beginning to feel like small beer.

Ginborn was indeed a pleasant and tranquil change. They were welcomed by Serene, the facilitator of the Love and Light Awareness week they had booked for. She showed them into a sparklingly clean bedroom in the Visitors' Centre. 'You both English?' she asked in a relaxed Californian drawl. 'Many of us here in Ginborn are, like me, American. It's good to have you with us. The Awareness week starts proper tomorrow morning. Have a good night. Morning meditation is at 7-30.'

Flowing and Maya settled in quite quickly and easily.

Life at Ginborn was all laid out for them. Meditation in Sanctuary at 7-30 a.m., breakfast between 8-00 and 8-45, Awareness Group workshops in the morning, helping out with community work in the afternoon to get an experience of love and light in action, then an evening of circle dance, astrology, community meetings, time for a walk by the craggy seashore or for silent communion in the still woods nearby.

For the more spiritually advanced, there was the challenge of working with the special energies of the Ginborn power-point. It was approached via a long avenue of stately pines, allegedly used by Druids, and leading from a deep dell. The dell was thought to have been the meeting-place for the last coven of local witches before they were summarily dispatched to a grisly death in what was one of the last such executions in Scotland. The path led through the woods to a small conical hill, which was ascended in ritualistic fashion by a serpentine path which spiralled anti-clockwise to the summit. Several noted Ginborners had experienced potent visions at the sacred mound, one American man having claimed to have been lifted off it into a space-ship in which he visited Sirius. As he seemed to have subsequently lost the faculty of intelligible speech, nothing was learnt of the details of his cosmic trip. And in spite of the fact that locals muttered darkly of overdoses of magic mushrooms, the Ginborners held such legends with great reverence.

Flowing's first approach to the sacred power-point, however, proved singularly disappointing. Her face was scratched by brambles, she twisted her ankle in a rabbit-hole and found no space for the privacy of visions as the top of the hill was teeming with American guests getting into the energies. Still, it seemed to be one of the keys to understanding Ginborn and she promised herself that she would visit the power-point more privately when things had quietened down.

But there proved to be no time over the next few days. Her agenda was packed and there seemed to be so much new learning to do. There now appeared to have been glaring omissions in the education she had received through eleven years of compulsory schooling. For no state school-teacher had breathed a word about the purpose of the planet on which they all lived, nor how humanity had emerged from the primal swamps during the age of Lemuria, had fallen prey to the sin of spiritual arrogance prior to the cleansing flood of Atlantis, and was at this point of history progressed beyond the age of Pisces ( the epoch of Christianity) to the dawning of the Age of Aquarius and group consciousness. No longer was God to be the stern judgmental Jehovah, the Christ-energy was to be released into each individual and centres such as Ginborn were working at grounding this beginning of humanity's initiation into Christ-consciousness.

Indeed powerful group-invocations were solemnly

pronounced at meditations where the planetary servants asked to be penetrated by Christ energy. The penetrations were certainly more refined and ethereal than the crude physical variety favoured by the Whambamers, though perhaps lacking a bit in kicks. However, Flowing and Maya were told that they were now operating at a much higher level than they might expect to find amongst those who chose to work from the lower chakras. And among the Ginborners, their cosy little family bungalows, their ordered daily existence, their quiet humour aligned to a serious sense of spiritual purpose, the two young women began to feel quite at home. True, most Ginborners were quite middle-aged and surprisingly upper-middle class compared with the Creeping Snake Camp followers. But being around the creature comforts and the stability of older, more settled people gave the two of them a feeling of rightness about things. They felt as if at last they had come home.

Indeed all was very peaceful and uplifting. The only thing that marred the quiet rhythms of their days was the occasional ear-piercing shriek of jet-engines. Ginborn was built right next to a RAF Strategic Strike Command base bristling to the teeth with nuclear warheads. Flowing was greatly surprised to learn that the Ginborn approach to their militaristic neighbours was one of unsimulated friendship. The base commander, Air Commodore Barnabas Blastattem, and his Wing-Commanders, could be seen periodically in the inner sanctums of the community attending chatty little tea-parties. Ginborn leading lights were invited over to the base every so often for any social function the base was holding. The whole approach, it was explained in response to Flowing's queries, was one of fostering good neighbourliness.

And certainly things flowed mellowly along at Ginborn. The community meetings were friendly exchanges, sparkling with sharpened wit and bonhomie. Even the community's rather frighteningly huge overdraft was the subject of light-hearted jest and interpersonal conflict seemed to have been eliminated. The passions, given free rein by the Whambamers, were nowhere in evidence. Flowing asked about this startlingly different feature of social life - what happened to all the personal gossip, back-biting and rancours that were so much a feature of Old-Age social interactions? 'Well,' Serene beamed 'here at Ginborn we are encouraged to work on the inner, to take our heavy issues into the Sanctuary and meditate on them, to transmute our own personal attachments and aggression, and release our fearful ego-positions. Just release things.' She exhaled lightly before continuing. 'In addition, many members counsel each other on real heavy stuff that comes up for them. They work in pairs to get rid of all the negative emotions in sessions together so that it won't be dumped at anyone who triggers those feelings on the outer. It really works.'

And certainly, from Flowing's observation of daily

life in the community, relationship-hassles didn't seem to flare up. She overheard what could have developed into a heated dispute being sorted out smoothly in the potting-shed. One of the gardeners, Rock, had discovered that another gardener, Angelus, had been taking time off to meet a woman-friend in the depths of the herbaceous border - it seemed he had been unfolding to her the intricacies of the devic realms at work in the garden (the devas were tiny nature-spirits with whom some of the pioneer Ginborners communed). In the course of his lesson, which seemed to involve lying totally relaxed, body totally exposed to the elements, they had squashed several prized and expensive floral specimens. 'Material here for a right old barney,' thought Flowing. 'Wonder how they'll handle this?'

In a calm voice, Rock had given her a fine demonstration of Ginborn conflict-resolution in action. 'Angelus, there's something I want to share with you. First, a point of awareness, it's against community rhythms to take time out during work for personal non-urgent agendas.' A serene silence ensued. So far, so good. He next turned to address the female miscreant only to come face-to- face with his own partner in a very recent and very meaningful relationship. For a moment, his lip quivered and Flowing thought he was going to lose it. Instead, he continued 'Another point of awareness - if one rolls on Shasta daisies, they do not tend to grow very well. I just want to let you both know of my feelings about this incident - it really pains me deeply. And I hope it won't happen again.' 'Thank you for sharing' the cuckolding couple chorused and Angelus added 'I really appreciate your honesty with us and your deep sharing. Rest assured that the incident won't be repeated.'

The matter was over and done with, without any unseemly self-justifications, denials, bickering or raising of voices. Nor were resentments being stored up unhealthily. It was all very impressive and such a contrast to the knee-jerk up-front let-it-all-hang-out emotional splurges of the Whambamers. Flowing and Maya felt more and more drawn to becoming members.

Nothing seemed to stand in their way. Maya handed over a large sum of money to cover their membership for an initial six month's trial and they both attended a two month Induction into New Age Esoterics. Ginborn somewhat prided itself on its role as a Mystery School and there was a continual flow-through of guests from all over the world ( though mainly from America, South Africa and Australia) to get in tune with New Age energies. The community had over the last few years become so popular that it now had well over three hundred members and had built a huge pyramidal Planetary Mandala Healing Dome where meditations were held every Full Moon.

The new members of the community were

gradually introduced into the world of guardian-angels, spirit-guides and, most surprisingly to Flowing, a group of Spiritual Masters supervising the whole show - they were known simply as the Hierarchy. It was held that prominent members of the community were in daily communion with the Hierarchy during meditations and that, acting on instructions from this Higher Source, decisions having a vital bearing on the future of the community, and indeed of the planet, were made.

For it turned out that Ginborn and its related New Age centres had a key part to play in the future planetary transformations that had to be made. It seemed it was the karma of Great Britain and the United States of America to lead the world in its spiritual re-awakening and to guide it through the twenty-first century. Many would-be members questioned the paradox of the glaring inconsistency between the role of these twin pillars of capitalist exploitation and their ascribed new spiritual role as world saviours. But it was explained by the Mystery School teachers that things on the inner weren't always as clear as they appeared on any straight judgement of objective details. For example, the country of South Africa was held by many Ginborners to hold much of the light on the dark continent and New Age centres had flourished there alongside the racist regime. In the long sweep of history, what countries were up to in the 21st century didn't give the whole picture.

Developments had to be looked at from the esoteric viewpoint and how they fitted into the Grand Design.

For it seemed the Hierarchy were privy to a Plan for the Planet Earth and its living cargo. Flowing tried assiduously to probe further to unearth more of this ultimate purpose. But her mentors only recommended her to study several very obscure texts: 'A Discourse on Spiritual Fire,' 'The Esoteric Principles and Practice of White Light Magic,' 'Group Initiation Into Christ Consciousness,' 'Francis Bacon and the Role of the Masters.' With sincere attempts to further her understanding, Flowing ploughed diligently through these weighty tomes. But the more she pressed forward, the further the secrets of the Grand Design seemed to retreat from her.

Although hundreds of pages long, she could distil nothing of real substance from her studious perusals. Perhaps her understanding wasn't yet up to it. Perhaps the time wasn't right for her to penetrate into the deepest core of the mysteries. After all, 'The Discourse on Spiritual Fire' did warn that, although the mysteries of life's true purpose were now to be shared with the whole of humanity, the process would take some time.

One thing that leapt from the pages of the 'Discourse on Spiritual Fire' and was starkly clear, however, was the esoteric view of nuclear energy. The dropping of the bombs on Hiroshima and Nagasaki was heralded as ushering in a great new age for humanity, one of new clear - nuclear - energy. At this,

Flowing's overtaxed mind revolted. She saw before her the mutilated bodies of Japanese children, an accusation to all of sentient humanity. New clear energy indeed!

She cross-questioned Serene. Serene spoke cautiously. 'Ah well, Flowing, you're really getting into the territory of the advanced initiates here. All I can tell you is that the Masters have not yet revealed which way forward humanity is to take, one of total transformation or one of total devastation. Here at Ginborn we like to think positively, to work on the inner with our own holocaust energy in order that outer holocausts can be prevented. But, of course, it may be part of the Plan for us all to be taken into the Light in one last blinding flash.' 'What?' Flowing gasped 'You mean that the Plan might favour nuclear annihilation?' 'Well' Serene serenely continued, as if unperturbed by the prospect of her own imminent fry-up, 'it might be the best way that humanity can take this giant leap forward into the Age of Aquarius. Our vibrations will all be immediately increased, and we will all be working on a higher plane together.' 'But what about the earth?' objected Flowing, 'she'll be totally ruined.' Serene agreed 'Yes, but that may be all part of the Plan. And beautiful as She is, it may be part of Her own evolution.' 'I'll need to think about all this' said Flowing.

And think she did. Humanity's vibrations needed to be increased. That was plain for all to see. Things couldn't go on the way they had been going for the last few decades. But she personally could think of much more enjoyable ways of raising her vibrations than being incinerated in a white-hot radio-active explosion or slowly sickening to death from poisonous fallout. She thought longingly of her ecstasies with Leaning Pine - but it seemed the Plan of the Masters eschewed such an enjoyable path to higher consciousness. And the trials of the Tantric group, still so fresh in her mind, showed that a bed of roses had its own share of tormenting thorns.

Her mind wrestled with these weighty issues for many a long hour. She questioned established and respected community-members on the subject, but, like Serene, they seemed strangely indifferent to their own personal future fate and that of the planet. Also, they seemed convinced that whatever the Plan turned out to be, it would all be for the best. Flowing finally came to the conclusion that, if she were going to fit in at Ginborn, she would have to spend more time in Sanctuary so that she, too, would be undisturbed by the possibility, nay even desirability, of a nuclear holocaust.

For she did hanker after such composure. In spite of the daily meditations, and a certain surface calmness in her feelings, she was still aware of the nagging little pain in her heart that told her all was not well. True, she was soon happily settled in her work in the Guest Department of Ginborn and she had a fascinating job meeting visitors from many parts of the world, visitors moreover who shared her hunger for spiritual fare; true, she enjoyed the varied activities of Ginborn and could follow up her blossoming interest in aromatherapy and study in the well-stocked esoteric library.

Moreover her friendship with Maya was developing into a deep bond and they spent many hours together sharing their daily experiences. But there was no doubt that she yearned still for Leaning Pine, or at least for a more physical love-bond than Ginborn at present afforded her. Although she met hordes of eager male seekers, not one had yet succeeded in freeing her from the spell that chained her to the distant and unavailable Leaning Pine. Ginborn worked consciously with love-heart energy and during the many hours of focussing on her heart-chakra and visualising being encircled in a healing rainbow of love, Flowing wondered how the forces she was conjuring with would eventually manifest in her life. She didn't have long to wait. Unbeknown to her conscious self, her daily spiritual attunements were bringing towards her a knight in a shining armour of Light.

It was in her capacity as receptionist of the Guest Department that Flowing first set eyes on Sir Percival. Revered by the Ginborners as a White Magician of the highest degree, Sir Percival visited the community at regular intervals, to bestow on members the cherished gift of his wisdom. His shock of blazing white hair, his aristocratic bearing and mien, his accents redolent with distinction and breeding, created round him a charmed circle. At his oracular deliveries in the Great Planetary Mandala Healing Dome aspirants hung on his every word and appreciative laughter greeted the merry jests which liberally accompanied his speeches. He was especially popular with the women of Ginborn, who, as with the Whambamers, were very prominent in the life of their group. Apart from his dashing style, he turned their heads by waxing long and lyrical on his conviction that it was of key importance for the future of the planet that Feminine energy was, as in olden times, restored to reverence. Sir Percival also had a great love for trees and had collected slides of magnificent specimens from all over the world. He spent much of his time travelling the planet giving lecture-tours, visiting threatened forests and generally acting as one of the chief overlords of the embryonic Network of Light.

It was thus, Flowing realised, a singular honour that Sir Percival chose to single her out as object of his special attentions. As she met him at Reception and accompanied him to his guest-bedroom, she was flattered by his obvious interest in her and the many questions he asked her about her life and the way he gallantly and archly held the doors open for her (an archaic approach forgiveable in a man of his age and background.) She was even more flattered when he asked Personnel Department if Flowing could be relieved of Guest Department duties for the week of his stay in order to act as his personal assistant. What an honour and what an opportunity to learn from this Great Master! Was she up to it? she wondered.

She presented herself to him rather nervously on the first morning of her new duties. She had attired herself in the soft flowing garb favoured by most Ginborn women members, with added care to her toilet. She had rinsed her cheeks in rosewater, washed her hair in rosemary fresh from the herb-garden and discreetly perfumed herself with Ylang Ylang, noted, she read afterwards on the label, for its powerful effects as an aphrodisiac. At the time, she had interrogated herself rigorously, wondering at her undue attention to her personal appearance that morning. Surely she wasn't trying to seduce Sir Percival? She hadn't even been aware of thinking of him as a possible suitor. But why had she unconsciously chosen the heady Ylang Ylang that morning rather than the modest Dewberry? Was she attracted to Sir Percival at a deep level or was she just the victim of stubbornly ingrained female conditioning that required her to make herself pleasing to a man of such obvious power? She couldn't tell.

Sir Percival was waiting graciously for her after breakfast. His light grey eyes roved up and down her appreciatively before he launched into a briefing of her busy schedule for the next few days. Flowing was to jot down his random impressions as he walked around as substance for his talks in the evening, she was to set up visits to key community departments for him, organise transport for several local visits and so on. What leapt out at her from the week's programme was that she was to accompany him and a few selected community members on a special ritual he was planning, to recharge the energies of the sacred power-point. This was to be the highpoint of his visit, held on his last night, and planned for then as it happened to be an eclipse of the moon. Her heart began to pound excitedly in anticipation of the night - surely this would be a major initiation for her, an initiation into realms hitherto the preserve of the Masters and their inner circle.

The week went by in a whirl of social arrangements, community business-meetings, trips to local forests and to the ancient well of St. Agnes to collect sacred water for the special ceremony. In between were precious half-hours snatched with Sir Percival to relax and reminisce. She spent all of her waking hours in his presence and as the days passed, she felt even more awed by the reality of his being than she had been at first by his reputation. His gallantry to her was most touching, he called her 'My dear', bought her little presents, and generally treated her like a heavenly princess walking on earth. Far from feeling like a used dogsbody catering for all the tedious organisational details of his visit, she felt privileged to have the honour of serving him. His behaviour towards her was invariably beyond reproach. In fact, it was so impeccable that she began to wish his code wasn't quite so strict. She could have done with a little squeeze on the hand from him or even an avuncular pat on the shoulder. But, she surmised, Sir Percival would undertake wooing most probably at the highest etheric level to begin with and she would have to be patient for any tangible signs of any possible love for her.

For by now, Flowing had become hopelessly infatuated with Sir Percival, he crystallised for her all that was noble and inspiring, he lived by lofty ideals and tirelessly worked for planetary transformation. Moreover, he fitted the bill as an idealised and unavailable father-figure she would trade any day for the boring prosaic reality of her own biological father. His only concern was whether he could grub up the pennies to cover the mortgage payments on their cramped little semi. Sir Percival was above all that. It was with gladness of heart that she served him.

The only time she was apart from him (except of course for the hours of his chaste sleep) were on the occasion of two of the many meetings he attended during his stay. The first was with the Community Accounts Department and left him, Flowing detected, momentarily a little deflated. But never one for succumbing to woe, he straight-away swung into action and made a couple of telephone calls, one to fix up a meeting the next day with Air Commodore Blastattem.

The next day, Flowing had to accompany Sir Percival to the railway station where they picked up a very smart austere-looking gentleman who looked all the world as if he had stepped off the pages of a spy-thriller. 'Good you could come so quickly, old boy. Blastattem's waiting' boomed Sir Percival cordially as they proceeded to the air base for a quiet little tea. 'You can take a break now, my dear' Sir Percival told Flowing as he ushered his visitor into the Air Commodore's office for this second private engagement. This meeting lasted some time but after a couple of hours, Sir Percival emerged looking his usual ebullient self. All the troubles printed heavily on his brow by the visit to Accounts had been magically erased. 'Decent chaps, my dear' he beamed at Flowing. 'It really pays to keep on neighbourly terms with them. Where to next?'

Next on the agenda was the community Karmic Key members meeting, which, in her capacity as Sir Percival's personal assistant, Flowing was allowed to attend. It was at these meetings that main community business was dealt with. The little administration office was crowded by the time she and Sir Percival joined the twelve members of the Karmic Key group. She listened in fascination as she witnessed how the Key group went about decision-making, from matters as diverse as replacement of linen in the Guest Department, to planning next summer's educational programme. Each item on the agenda was thoroughly aired and if intractable differences surfaced, the group observed a few minutes silence - within that time a compromise invariably seemed to emerge. Flowing was once again impressed.

About one matter, however, there was instant unanimity. A local peace group had written to the community announcing a big all-Scotland Peace march, supported by all Scottish churches, and opposed to nuclear weaponry. The letter requested that Ginborn host twenty or so participants for a night as they marched south —all the available church halls had been made available but were not enough to accommodate all the marchers. The Karmic Key group secretary was summarily instructed to write to the peace group to say ( lovingly) that Ginborn saw itself as a centre demonstrating a new way of life, and that as a community they were not in favour of the old-style confrontational type of approach to politics. The community favoured only positive causes and didn't agree with harping on in an endless spate of negativity protesting things.

Moreover, they held that it was serving humanity more to model a new peaceful lifestyle than to keep on in anger protesting against the old. However, the letter was to finish by sending Peace March Scotland the blessings and healing force of Limitless Love and Truth, the presiding Angel of Ginborn. The whole epistle was to be neatly rounded off with the words of a chant that Flowing had heard once or twice at

Ginborn and of which she had not, until this moment, appreciated the subtleties:

> *'I forgive myself for all __apparent__ injustice*
> *And for my part in starting it.'*

In the moment of silence that followed this particular piece of business, Flowing tried to process what she had just heard. Surely, to establish liberty for all, courageous individuals and groups had had to make a stand against slave-traders? Moreover, how would the Ginborners react if they had been placed in pre-war Nazi Germany - would their spirituality require them to turn a blind eye to current atrocities and focus only on building alternatives? Was the awful reality of Treblinka to be labelled merely an apparent injustice, apparent presumably because it was redressing some old karmic score and was she personally responsible, along with all the peace activists and the rest of humanity, for initiating and inflicting such torments. She made a mental note to think this through later on and dragged her attention back to the current sharing on the colour of the new drapes for Sanctuary.

It was on their way back through the dusk that Flowing and Sir Percival bumped into a compact little figure hurrying towards Sanctuary. With a start, Flowing recognised Marianne, beneficiary like herself of Aurora's prosperity techniques. They were both pressed for time but she learned that Marianne was thinking of joining the community. She had made so many changes since Aurora's workshop, life was dramatically exciting for her now. As Flowing regarded her plump face animated by excitement at meeting up with a fellow-traveller, she felt a sudden stir of affection for this woman old enough to be her mother yet with the courage to be experimental about her life. Her own mother would no doubt pass her ending days not so much as branching out to buy a new brand of coffee, Flowing reflected.

By contrast, here was Marianne taking charge of her life in bold new directions. She did look rather tired though. Marianne mentioned that she had in fact been feeling a bit under-the-weather physically of late and it was with genuine concern that Flowing advised her to go to the community's Body and Soul healing group. She decided to try and keep in touch with Marianne over the next few weeks. But now, back to Sir Percival and the arrangements for that night's healing ritual on the power-point. Flowing strolled beside Sir Percival's gesticulating figure as he listed things she needed to bring - some flares to guide them up the bushy little path round the power-point, a flagon containing the healing water from St Agnes' well and some crystals. She was to meet him in the little dell dead on nine.

It was a wild blustery night that greeted Flowing as she pushed her way against the wind through the trees to the dell. Huddled against the trees she distinguished a small knot of figures. Sir Percival's tall silhouette was immediately recognisable, draped in an imposing royal-blue cloak. 'Here, my dear' he gasped at her through the wind. She billowed towards him. In the pitch-black and propelled by an extra-powerful gust, she lurched bodily into his slight frame and felt with a start how skeletal and insubstantial he was, truly a wraith-like warlock. She felt a tiny frisson of fear mingling with her awe and love for him.

'First of all, we have to cleanse this spot of all accumulated energy, of all vile workings from the past' bellowed Sir Percival. 'Form a circle together.' As the circle came together, Flowing had a second shock. She was the only woman amongst how many men? - she counted - twelve, plus herself, equalled thirteen. As she gradually discerned their features, she recognised the others present as male stalwarts of the community, all respected initiates, she suspected. What was she doing among them?

It soon became clearer. Sir Percival charged her to bring him the sacred water and he sprinkled it grandly in the four directions, invoking Saint Gabriel, Saint Raphael, Saint Michael and others whose names were lost in the chilly blast. 'We are here tonight' he proceeded 'to exorcise this sacred spot from the blackest of abominations, from the darkest of energies, from the most wicked of paths.' Flowing trembled. What could he mean? What exactly had happened on this spot?

'It is here' Sir Percival's tone took on a note of hysterical outrage 'that local witches summoned up diabolical energies in the service of lower agencies. It is here that the work of the Masters was vilely rejected. It is here that the forces of Darkness still lurk within the bosom of our dear Ginborn, doing daily battle with our noble servants of the Light.' Finally his voice reached a falsetto climax. 'It is here that they violated nature with lewd sexual orgies,' he ejaculated. His last utterance was accompanied by an involuntary shudder of disgust. For a split-second, Flowing glimpsed his face etched in the darkness by the fleeting appearance of the moon. His eyes were beaming a cold fire. Flowing's fear suddenly mounted to a spasm of terror. What was Sir Percival up to? Could he be planning to counteract the evils of women's sexual orgies with their devilish consort by some propitiation involving herself? Surely it was no accident that the sex-ratios in his rite were reversed. But no, she told herself firmly, Sir Percival was a sworn devotee of Limitless Love and Truth - he could perpetrate no foul deed upon her, physically or psychically.

And sure enough, in a moment, things appeared reassuringly safe again, albeit a little bizarre. After further furious pacings of the circle and further emphatic sprinkling of holy water, Sir Percival closed his circle with instructions to follow him up the avenue to the path spiralling round the power-point.

He strode out in the van, with Flowing directed to bring up the rear. As they advanced through the storm,

Sir Percival glanced anxiously at his watch. The lunar eclipse was due at 9.57. He hadn't bargained on such adverse weather and his sacred rite had to commence at the exact moment of the eclipse. The gale had by now reached terrifying proportions, pines lashed by the wind groaned ominously over their heads and appeared to a by now rather numb Flowing to be attempting to flail out at them. 'Tis the work of the elementals' Sir Percival rasped through clenched teeth, 'they had them in their thrall. Sons of Light, gird your loins and forward to the summit.'

It was a perilous ascent, bodies battling against the tornado, hair lashing faces, feet losing their grip on the rutted path, torches constantly guttering, plunging them momentarily into darkness. But, at length, miraculously, they were standing on the summit, in the protection of a small grove of birch trees. 'We've made it' boomed Sir Percival triumphantly. 'Splendid effort, everyone. Now for our recharging to begin.' He peered again at his watch and scanned the skies. Again the moon appeared for a moment between the scudding clouds. She was now beginning to eclipse. 'The time is right' he rasped ' the time when the dark lunar energies are held at bay, engulfed by the solar force, when the power of Light over Dark is at its peak. '

He again marked out a circle with loud imprecations and imperious gestures in the air. 'Be with us, Angelic Beings' he commanded 'as we recharge this sacred site, aligning it to its true spiritual purpose, in the service of the Plan.' He began a frantic pacing of the circle, muttering. Then his voice broke into a crisp firm injunction:

*'May purpose guide the little wills of men,*

*The purpose which the Masters know and serve,*

*Let Light and Love and Power restore the Plan on Earth.'*

'Men's little wills?' Flowing furrowed her brow. Sir Percival must be talking esoterically rather than referring to hang-ups about sexual endowment - or did it all come down to the same thing in the end? she wondered irreverently for a second. Sir Percival did not elaborate. He rubbed his brow with sacred water and fulminated further, gathering his billowing cloak masterfully around him.

But if what was going on was veiled in obscurity for Flowing, Sir Percival's male acolytes seemed to have perfect understanding of the intent of his exhortations. As one man, they closed their eyes and assumed expressions of intense concentration. Freezing rain bucketed down their faces but they remained stoically and impassively at their spiritual posts. 'Whatever is going to happen?' Flowing wondered. She had promised herself a powerful ritual that would finally give her a glimpse of the work of the Hierarchy. But, in reality, nothing seemed to be developing. Sir Percival continued to pace round the circle, sodden hair plastered unflatteringly over his noble brow. The other men continued to stand stock still, intent on some mighty Herculean task, it seemed. The minutes dragged by. A large night-bird flew by and deposited evidence of its animality on the face of one of the loyal brotherhood of Light - he remained unmoved. He continued on his devoted meditations, not even batting an eyelid or pausing to wipe the excrement from his face.

Flowing's feet were by then miserably cold and sodden. Her hands were aching with the strain of trying to hold the flare upright against the gale. But still Sir Percival paced and raved, occasionally casting his hands up to the heavens with an extra-earnest imprecation. 'Lords of Light' he intoned, 'may we be willing servants of your cosmic fire.' The wind whipped one of the flares into a flaming blaze and in its glow his face once again looked quite unlike itself, a death-mask with eyes beaming out a laser-like ray.

Flowing's heart missed a beat at the sight and a truly alarming thought hit her. Perhaps the Hierarchy in the heavens wasn't so divorced from that on earth, perhaps they might be quite closely connected, they might even be working together hand in glove? After all, hadn't Sir Percival and the rest of the Ginborn elite seemed rather over-pally with neighbours like Air Commodore Blastattem and the RAF types, whilst having little or no time for other neighbours who were antinuclear activists? Was their spiritual hierarchy just an invention of the elite planetary brotherhood to further their temporal power games? And was the constant invocation of cosmic light and fire allied with reverence for blinding white fiery nuclear blasts? Her mind began to bend nightmarishly.

But her attention was summarily drawn back to Sir Percival. His ritual was evidently now at its peak. Fumblingly, he was involved in the task of trying to implant crystals in the earth with his bare hands. For several minutes he struggled with the stubbornly tenacious roots till in the end he had succeeded in thrusting the crystals under some clods. The effort left him limp and exhausted and looking immensely old. 'I impregnate the Earth with the energies of the Christ' he moaned.

Flowing's eyes were riveted on him. His face visibly chilled by the temperature, his bones shivering with the cold, he seemed suddenly not a majestic magician but a pathetic old gentleman engaged in eccentric spiritual games that might endanger the health of a man of his age and frame. He was going to need a good hot bath when he got back, Flowing found herself fussing. The vision of him feebly struggling with the elements had re-opened her heart to him and all horrendous suspicions had fled. 'How could I have thought such disloyally monstrous thoughts of the old boy?' she lectured herself. 'After all, he is dedicated to Limitless Love and Truth. Even if he does spend time with the Air Commodore, it is most likely a selfless task, tedious hours of chat trying to win him over from war-mongering, to guide him onto the sacred path. Here he is braving the elements to try to save the world he loves'. 'Yes, love' murmured Sir Percival - 'the key to our Path. Let us return, Light warriors, our work is done.'

They turned on their heels and proceeded on their descent. This was a good deal easier than their climb up, though not without its hazards. One such hazard brought Flowing, however, to a sudden and dramatic re-assessment of Sir Percival. It happened on the final twist of the path. Sir Percival tripped on a root and careened unceremoniously into a gorse bush. This setback evoked such a volley of vulgar oaths that Flowing for a moment questioned his noble antecedents. She also wondered wryly whether, though unmoved in theory by the prospect of being consumed in nuclear infernos, he could in actuality deal with the physical reality of such a scenario when he seemed hardly able to handle a slight brush with a bush. But, in a moment, he had regained his cool and acted as if his plebeian outburst had not occurred. At length, they reached the bottom of the hill. Sir Percival bade his brotherhood goodnight.

Then he turned eagerly to Flowing. 'How was it for you, my dear?' he queried. She was caught completely off her guard. 'Damp, cold, miserable and ultimately boring' came to the tip of her tongue. Certainly if the witches had specialised in the energies of climax, Sir Percival seemed to have a forte for anticlimax. 'I - I - I' was all she could say. 'Quite so, my dear' he finished for her 'tremendously powerful. Did you feel the earth move?' Such was Flowing's indoctrinated reverence for aristocrats that all she could do was nod assent. Privately she sighed to herself, the scales had fallen from her eyes. Sir Percival was no longer her champion on a steed of Light, he was just a rather vainglorious old man with an immense fear of women's spiritual power and autonomy. Whether or not his ultimate spiritual aims were questionably married to hidden political ones she would have to investigate further. For the moment, she had had more than enough of Sir Percival. He could organise his own bath.

# CHAPTER 6

# THE MASTER PLAN EXPOSED

The morning after the letdown of the Lunar Eclipse ritual, Flowing woke with numb despair. Would she ever become privy to the secrets of the Master Plan? It seemed not. Moreover, she was now alerted to possible sinister connections between the guiding-lights at Ginborn and the invisible hands that steered the economy. For how else could she explain the fact that Ginborn always managed to pull itself back from the brink of financial crisis and was year-by-year acquiring expensive properties? - radical communities offering a real political challenge to society were distinguished by a sore struggle for pennies. What exactly was the true purpose of Ginborn? Was the Brotherhood of Light just another male-identified powergroup with token female members and the hidden aim of preserving the status quo, even, if necessary, with nuclear fire-storms? Though superficially everything in the Ginborn garden seemed just lovely, Flowing had definitely begun to smell a rat.

She took her sentiments straightaway that morning to Maya. She described in detail what she had experienced that week and where she was left at the end of it all. Maya listened attentively. Then she summed up for Flowing. 'Well, Flowing, if Sir Percival has done nothing else, at least he's got you over Leaning Pine.' 'Why yes' Flowing assented. For it was true. For the first time in weeks she felt free from daily yearning. There was still the dull ache in her heart but now it didn't seem as if only Leaning Pine, or more recently, Sir Percival, could assuage its grip. Surely her next step must be to dig deeper into the facts behind the founding of Ginborn. It was likely that only a few people knew the full story and that the rest of the members accepted the official line - Ginborn was about Love and Light - its purpose being to transform society from an unregenerate grasping materialism into a new order based on a refined spirituality aligned with the higher purposes of the Plan of the etheric Hierarchy.

Over the next few weeks Flowing proceeded carefully to ferret around. Elevated by Sir Percival's trust in her, she found that she had gone up a few notches in the community hierarchy. And that formerly reticent key members now seemed more willing to give free rein to their tongues with her. But it seemed they all, to a man, had just about as much real contact with the Hierarchy as she herself did. She even sought an interview with founding members. But again she drew a curious blank. Even there she found no convincing proof that the original impetus for Ginborn was truly divinely inspired and connected with some grand spiritual design.

So how could the Ginborners claim they were aligned with the Plan of the Masters if none of them seemed to know the least bit about the plan, let alone any specifics of it? As the Karmic Key group purported to be in constant communion with the Hierarchy, its decisions on all matters were given spiritual legitimacy. And who could prove or disprove this spiritual connection and how? In the end, all she could accuse the Ginborn elite of was a certain rock - like smugness, and a lack of discrimination as to which of their neighbours they graced with invitations to tea. She had no proof at all of anything more ominous. Still, she had a strong intuition that something was deeply wrong.

By the end of a few weeks they were both fed up with the futility of their quest. They took to spending many hours together in the sweltering sauna, lazing in the woods or frolicking on the sea-shore, pondering the meaning of life at Ginborn and whether or not it was truly a community worthy of so much of their daily energy. They were joined on many occasions by Marianne, who had decided not to join Ginbom outright, but to enrol in a three-month Living in the Light group. Over the weeks, they became a warm close threesome, regarded now by the Ginborners with some suspicion as nascent dissenters.

It was at this point that Maya became aware of the Mayan factor. One day she appeared before her friends flourishing a batch of papers and burbling excitedly.

Piles of leaflets had appeared in the Ginborn community-centre announcing the actual timing of the dawn of the new millennium. It seemed that this was to be ushered in on certain key dates and at certain key sites all over the planet. They were listed in the voluminous sheaves of paper which began daily to inundate the community. It all turned on the secrets of the Mayan calendar of the Aztecs, which predicted a cosmic trigger-point when the planetary energy would shift gear to a much more advanced level. In Aztec lingo, the ninth Hell cycle was coming to an end; Quetzalcoatl, the feathered serpent, would make a second coming, remove his jade mask and reveal his true nature, ushering in a new age of peace. Moreover, Hopi Indian legend coincidentally claimed that on the same key dates, 144,000 enlightened Sun Dance teachers would help awaken the rest of humanity.

The claims leaping forth from the welter of pages were truly staggering - and included descriptions of the U.S. West Coast breeding programme for unicorns and of cabbages that were not only huge but could walk, talk and tap dance. All was backed up by a screed of tightly-typed instructions, exact times of cosmic-consciousness shifts timetabled with fanatical precision, and pleas that readers would align themselves to shift gear by getting together with other would-be enlightened Sun Dance teachers to bring the earth into a galactic synchronisation-phase. This was the first time in 23,412 years that nine planets would be aligned in the configuration of a Grand Trine, creating an energy greater than any experienced on earth to-date.

The alternative, the papers warned, would be truly appalling - readers who didn't join in could consider themselves consorts of the Anti-Christ and would probably be zoned off to a really deadly planetary layer. Moreover, Armageddon would not be forestalled and in the near future, we would all die hideously. When it came down to it, if you had any aspirations at all to be on any kind of spiritual path, then you had to be at Palenque in El Tule on the Gemini New Moon on 24th May at 11.47 a.m. holding a vibration of peace or at Lake Titicaca on the Cancer Full Moon 31st December at 6.35 p.m. celebrating Immaculate and Joyous Birth, or possibly at the Great Pyramid on the Libran New Moon, 7th October, 9.40 p.m. helping the tree of Immortal Law and Justice to take root.

It seemed at last as if the details of the Cosmic Plan had finally been fleshed out for all to see. And the gifted mortals (or were they, as some of them claimed, immortal?) who had channelled the minutiae of the Plan, metaphysical hermits, occult mathematicians and sons of magicians, were in charge of assembling all the enlightened souls for the grand project of activating the second Great Fire Serpent. The most crucial date they termed the Harmonic Convergence and was scheduled for 11.03 a.m. on August 17th in three weeks time.

Even the Ginborners, inured as they were to superficially preposterous claims by years of over-exposure, could not fail to be moved. Should it be Table Mountain on the 15th or Kangwha Bay on the 3rd? The whole community was in a fever. The waves of the craze also washed over our three friends. By now bogged down in their search for the ultimate meaning of life at Ginborn, the new bizarrely extraordinary project began to take a grip. If they had failed to find the key to the Plan at Ginborn, perhaps they should give this grand endeavour a try.

The discussions they held on the subject were intense and heated at times. This was the fourth new venture Flowing would be embarking on. She had been told at each step on her path to go forward in daily faith, that all was for the best. But at this point on her journey, even her generous reserves of optimism were reaching exhaustion-point. However, it was difficult not to be affected by the daily increasing excitement of the Ginborners. Foregoing their usual placid routines, the whole community was at sixes and sevens, hyping themselves up for the synchronisation of the cosmic-gear change. The etheric hotlines were busy as members hastily enquired of spirit-guides as to exactly where they were meant to be on the fateful hour, aeroplane timetables were being furiously consulted. Dolphins had been sighted dis-sporting themselves in the nearby bay - an occurrence rare beyond imagination in recent years and this was taken as a sign of impending momentous events.

Maya and Marianne fast became caught up in the suspense of planning for the first of the 93 activation phases. And gradually Flowing was won round, finally convinced by another portent that had rocked the community. Whilst deep in meditation in the Great Mandala Healing Dome, several Ginborners has heard powerful hissing noises which they knew at once to be the summons of the Great Fire Serpent. (The local plumber, who was tinkering with the perennially faulty boiler - fitted by a pioneer Ginborner under direct guidance from Shamballa - knew better and tittered to himself down deep in the vaults of the Dome. But he chose to keep his knowledge to himself. Spectating the antics of the Ginborners was a free local past-time and tales of their daft deeds whiled away the long winter nights).

So it was that late one evening, the three friends stood poised over a map of the world, pondering their position on the first and most important consciousness gear-shift date, the Harmonic Convergence. Armed with Maya's cheque-book, the world was their oyster. But the very range of choices available made the decision even harder, especially for Flowing and Marianne who had never before had the finance for such exotic voyages. Eventually they concluded that the only possible way to reach a decision was to plunge a pin at random on the map. Maya was blindfolded and turned around a magic seven times. The others watched spell-bound as her hand falteringly plunged the marker onto the map - it landed only a millimetre away from one of the central power-points of the planet, the Temple of Delphi in Greece, regarded by the ancients as the navel of the world.

Two weeks later found them camped with over a hundred similarly-inspired companions on the terraces at the foot of the sheer cliffs that veered above the little village of Delphi. It was as near to the Sanctuary of the Earth Mother as they could get. The ancient site had provided them with many long absorbing hours of exploration. It was, guidebooks agreed, one of the most beautiful landscapes of the world: perched on the side of Mount Parnassus, the sanctuary of Apollo overlooked the gorge of Pleistos, the Sacred Plain with its carpet of olive trees reaching to the Gulf of Itea in the distance.

When the heat rose to infernal levels, the visitors took themselves off for a refreshing swim in the luminous waters of the Gulf. They bought their daily fare at Delphi whose citizens, although reputed to have lived for centuries by ruthlessly exploiting pilgrims to the oracle, nevertheless seemed unstintingly kind and helpful. In the cool of the evening, the visitors rambled round the relics on the site, the temples of Athena, the Gymnasium, the Temple of Apollo, the Sacred Way ending in the crossroads of the tripods, savouring as they went the mystique of the many votary objects that had survived the ravages of time, fires and earthquakes. It was all something of a knock-out.

Not that the enlightened Sundancers needed any extra stimulus, their own adrenalin high was powerfully self-propelling. They congregated daily round their central camp-fire, complete with typed transcripts. They were mostly American and it seemed had been preparing themselves for months for the event. Each of them had felt overpoweringly drawn to Delphi and the air was full with the sounds of their chimes, their mantras and their hundredth discussion of the hundredth monkey phenomenon. At intervals, they joined hands and performed vibrational toning, moaning aaaah for seven minutes at a time until their whole bodies vibrated. Many of the men had strange apparatuses, Heavi Hemi Sinks, strapped around their heads. It seemed these devices were brain-machines, emitting pulsed sound at frequencies to send out waves of calmness and higher powers to the mind of the wearer. Several enthusiasts were avidly debating to which specific frequency they should set their machines at the moment of gear-change. Daily they discussed how the group should celebrate the g.s.t. (as the cosmic gear synchronisation came to be known).

As the day approached for this joint momentous leap in consciousness, they had come to a decision. After a day's fast, they would ritually costume themselves, paint their faces with sacred signs, and as g.s.t. approached, process in gay array along the Sacred Way to the Castilian spring. This was located in a ravine reputed to be the lair of a serpent Python, possibly an ancient relation of their own now beloved Second Fire Serpent. There they were to re-enact the sacred marriage of Quetzalcoatl in a specially constructed Bridal Chamber. Two people were chosen as bride and bridegroom. The bride was the most adorable young woman, probably not yet out of her teens. Incongruously, the group chose as groom a rather ancient, unsightly, but influential American Sundancer who prided himself on his shamanic prowess.

From then on, everyone threw themselves into preparations, putting together fabulous costumes, decked out in all the flimmery the local shops could muster. The camp-site began to assume the air of a gaudily decorated carnival. Each member felt drawn to a particular role, Flowing, with her penchant for aromatic herbs, prepared infusions to fumigate the bridal chamber. Maya sewed coloured sequins and feathers onto the outfit of the feathered serpent. Marianne, who was still feeling very poorly physically, retreated to the relative cool of the local library where a huge archive of rarely consulted dusty volumes told her of the past sacred mysteries in which Delphi was steeped. Or she rested in the moist stone recesses near the altar of Hygieia, Goddess of Health, contemplating the myriad statuettes of woman-deities.

As each passing minute brought them closer to g.s.t., the atmosphere in the makeshift camp reached delirium-level. Only Marianne seemed unmoved by the frenetic vibes. Indeed at times she seemed positively taciturn, even infected by a touch of negativity towards the rest of the camp and its endeavours. Flowing and Maya put her mood down to her obvious poor state of health. But on the eve of the great day, she drew her friends aside and asked them to accompany her to a quiet spot. She had something she urgently wanted to tell them.

In the solemn silence of a ruined temple, surrounded by terracota statues of Athena Zosteria (the Goddess girding herself for battle), she requested them to sit with her for a few minutes and attend to the stillness that pervaded the temple of stone. Her steadiness, poise and depth suddenly seemed to her companions a strange and salutary contrast to the manic energy of the camp they had just left. She started to speak and it was as if a door fleetingly opened and poured forth a blaze of illumination into long-dark chambers of their minds.

Firstly, Marianne told them that she was feeling totally alienated from the whole Harmonic Convergence enterprise. For her researches in the local archives had given her a glimpse of the awesome powers of the site, powers which she felt the American jet-setting crew hadn't the reverence to approach in the proper spirit. She felt almost as if the temple, sacred to the Earth Mother, was about to be violated by the impending rite imposed from another culture, a rite with no real connection to the dedicated purpose of the sacred shrine at Delphi. Her voice became darkly angry as she spoke of a prior rape of the site.

She had learnt that, from at least the middle of the second millennium BC, the ancient Goddess Gaia had been worshipped at Delphi. The Earth Goddess was famed for her delivering of oracles and was associated with her daughter, Themos, who presided over the Delphic site after her. The site of her oracle was situated near a cave guarded by the monstrous serpent, Python. The priestesses of the cult sat in the cave near a fissure in the rocks from which emerged subterranean fumes which induced a state of oracular frenzy. This was aided by the drinking of a heady brew concocted from the narcotic leaves of the local laurel. The prophetesses were held in great awe and were consulted to give guidance as to the balanced regulation of the ancient society, a regulation in accordance with the rhythms of the Earth Mother. Reverence for the words of the oracle ensured a stable peaceful society that had lived in harmony with the earth for countless generations.

All this had ended towards the end of the 9th century BC when warrior hordes swept in from the East, seized the holy shrine, and adapted it to their own warlike culture. They renamed it the Temple of Apollo and consulted it mainly to sort out disputes or to further the temporal aims of the fiercely militaristic city-states that jockeyed for prominence in the area. Use of the laurel leaves was banned, allegedly because it drove the priestesses into paroxysms of violence in which they might even go so far as to hunt down any men unfortunate enough to be in the vicinity and put them to a bloody death.

Marianne paused. Flowing and Maya had been listening intently. Her words had made a deep impression. But what Marianne was next to announce shook them to the core. 'Tomorrow I'm not going to take part in the g.s.t. jamboree. I am walking up to the Corycian cave a few miles from here. It was held to be sacred to the nymphs and the old cult of Gaia. I am going to drink an infusion of laurels. I've got them already.' In her palm rested a handful of silvery grey leaves, superficially ordinary enough, but apparently capable of revealing potent secrets.

At first, Flowing and Maya were at a loss for thoughts and words. What Marianne had told them was powerfully fascinating and set off reverberations at a deep level. But they were 20th century women and talk of deadly pythons, laurel leaves and oracular frenzies had a darkly dangerous ring to them, unlike the exotic but suddenly cosy-seeming Quetzalcoatl wedding rite - the worst that could happen there was a last minute attack of cold feet on the part of the Quetzal bird and some consternation for a jilted Coatl serpent abandoned at the altar, or that a union took place that was mismatched and would send some feathers flying.

But anything could befall Marianne if she dared to dabble into mysteries dubbed by men as out of bounds to mortals. After all, did she have the right dose? she could poison herself miles from any doctor. Marianne reassured them that she had gone into the matter thoroughly and she stood firm in her resolve. She was going to the cave next day. They were free to join her if they liked, in fact, she would welcome it. There would still be time for them to rejoin the Harmonic Convergence group at the g.s.t. of 1.03 p.m. local time.

There was absolutely no point in trying to dissuade Marianne. So, next morning, out of concern for her welfare, Flowing and Maya joined her in the early morning mists on the long trek up the mountain to the Corycian cave. Though they didn't say much, they both felt a grim foreboding. Their disquiet increased as they crouched with Marianne in the eerie darkness of the cave. What if something dreadful happened to Marianne? It would take them at least an hour to summon help. Marianne, for her part, seemed as steady as the rocks of the cave. She raised to her lips a flagon containing the ancient brew she had prepared and quaffed it in one draught. 'Know thyself' she murmured.

Silence fell. They all sat in anticipation of the outcome. The silence continued. An hour passed. Then a low moan broke from Marianne's lips, her face became ashen and her body started to tremble. An expression of stunned realisation gripped her face. But still she uttered not a word. Flowing and Maya waited in vain for the pronouncement of the oracle.

Then suddenly Marianne seemed seized by an almighty force. She heaved herself to her feet, emitted a piercing shriek, threw her hands in the air and rushed headlong out of the cave. Hot on the pursuit, Flowing and Maya stumbled after her but on reaching the entrance to the cave, Marianne's figure was visible fast disappearing down the track that led to Delphi. Hurry as they might, impelled by anxiety for Marianne, they could not catch up with her. Such was their speed that within half an hour they were back at the Sundancers' camp, dishevelled, breathless and distraught. At first, they could not find Marianne. But eventually they tracked her down to the temple of Athena. A strange guttural voice warned them away. 'Leave me alone! Leave me alone!' In the circumstances, they thought it best if they obeyed. Marianne did after all appear to be physically undamaged by the brew.

All around them the last-minute preparations for g.s.t. were in full swing. The participants were robing themselves in costumes appropriately splendid for the celebration of the marriage of a god. The bridal pair looked magnificent, in costumes of avian and reptilian features. Many hours had been spent in embellishing the Bridal Chamber near the Castilian spring where the wedding was to be enacted. The bower was woven from branches of nearby groves, intertwined with a display of dazzling flowers. The time was fast approaching. Flowing and Maya faced a decision. Should they go on with the show and trust that Marianne would be alright?

As all seemed deadly quiet in the Temple of Athena and they couldn't fail to be caught up in the flurry of last-minute wedding preparations, they found themselves at 12.50 assembled with the Sundancing team at the Castilian spring, costumed as dancing birds. All around them stood others in beautiful array, but none so striking as the bridal pair. They stood in the blazing noonday sun, the man splendid in a feathered costume sparkling with a million sequins, the woman in a tightly woven skin suit, whose diamond patterns simulated a snake. Nobody would have guessed the senility of the groom. And nobody watching could fail to have been moved. The group processed towards the bridal bower chanting powerfully. The group energy was moving towards a crescendo. The couple stepped towards the door. They turned to face the assembled crowd. From the threshold they waved to them. They were to enter the bower and consummate their union at the appointed g.s. t. whilst the rest of the group stood chanting in a circle outside.

But the grand consummation of the marriage of Quetzalcoatl was not to be. For suddenly a wild distraught figure leapt out of nowhere into the midst of the group. It was a woman, naked, hair flying in all directions, body daubed with red ochre. Gazing wildly about her, she strode towards the bridal chamber, thrust aside the royal couple and forced her way roughly into the tiny bower. It was exactly 1.03 p.m., gear synchronisation time, when the group assembled outside heard the unmistakable sound of somebody passing water. The bridal bed was being defiled. A shocked silence held the group. From inside the bower now came sounds of gathering rage, of things being flung in all directions, of yells and curses. Finally, the woman's figure appeared again in the doorway. She stood stock still for a second gazing at the assembly. There was truly something splendid about her standing there in all her elemental being. Then with one last furious gesture, she flounced off down the slope as fast as she had come. 'The grandmother energy' gasped an elderly male Sundancer. 'Marianne' murmured Flowing and Maya.

Leaving the group noisily trying to resurrect their ritual, the two friends took off down the slopes after Marianne. They found her as they expected lying in the Temple of Athena, exhausted but triumphant-looking. 'Whatever possessed you?' they hurled at her. 'You've ruined the Gear Synchronisation.' 'Yes, I know' she returned. 'And I'm glad.' But no more would she say. She continued to lie holed up in the Temple of Athena.

Meanwhile Flowing and Maya thought it wise to

pack up their belongings with all possible speed and get themselves and Marianne out of the Sundance camp before the rest of the group returned. Working at lightning speed, they stuffed their belongings into bags, dismantled their tents, and finally dragged the still silently glowing Marianne from the Temple. Within a few minutes, they had washed, dressed and groomed her. She now no longer appeared an ancient possessed fury but a rather dazedly tired suburban matron. They propelled her between them down the little road to the Delphi bus stop. 'We've got to get out of here fast' muttered Flowing. 'But where to?' Maya wailed.

# CHAPTER 7
## REBIRTH INTO REALITY

Where to in fact seemed to be largely dictated by the ensuing turn of events. For on the trip from Delphi to the nearest airport, it became clear that Marianne was seriously ill. She complained of low fever, dull aches and dizziness. Moreover, dark blotches appeared on her skin. Her friends at first attributed her malaise to the after-effects of the narcotic leaves. But Marianne told them that she had been experiencing these symptoms for quite some weeks now and they were daily getting worse. And so it was that they headed straight back to London and an urgent health check-up for Marianne.

Within twenty-four hours they had been transported from the realms of ancient ruins, holy relics, outlandish outfits and bizarre rituals to the harsh strip-lighting glare, efficient and organised uniformed bustle of a hospital waiting-room, from one strange scene to another. Moreover, the news about Marianne proved very bad. The worst was suspected and she had to stay in hospital for further checks. Within a few days, the worst was confirmed. Marianne had advanced blood-cancer. The medics were gearing up for a radiation and chemical assault on her system.

Flowing and Maya were at first utterly downcast by the grim tum of events. Just a few days previously they had been happily anticipating mind-bending planetary miracles, now here they were dealing with the possibility of the imminent death of a friend. For they were both now very fond of Marianne and this affection enabled them easily to forgive her recent sabotage of the G.S.T. Besides, it was clear to them now, Marianne's disturbed outbreak had most probably been due to ill-health.

Marianne's reaction to the facts of her illness, however, pre-empted any displays of sympathy. For she insisted on rising from her bed, then she discharged herself from hospital and rejoined her friends. They were all staying with friends of Maya' s in a large central London house. Marianne was clear that she did not want to undergo the ordeal of 21st-century medicine. But what was the alternative?

The three friends poured over Natural Healing directories, following up leads from contacts as to which of the hosts of holistic healers would best be able to help Marianne. Over the next few weeks, she embarked on one health-cure after another. She was recommended by a dietary consultant to embrace a strict diet of raw fare, supplemented by mega-doses of mega-expensive vitamin and mineral supplements. She went for weekly acupuncture and reflexology treatments, aromatherapy, colour and light healing, Reiki, crystal healing, Shiatzu, iridology, the list went on. Finally she even descended to several hideously embarrassing sessions at Insides Out, the centre for colonic irrigation treatments.

Through all this she was bombarded by intuitive diagnosticians with costly courses of affirmations to address the root cause of her illness, which it seemed resided in her thoughts. But varied though their approaches were, nearly all the healers charged very big fees. Her health-consultants grew daily richer through her illness and had to expend much time and energy in their healers' support groups - there they worked at releasing guilt over profiting from the illness of others and overcoming their resistance to prosperity. All the while, Marianne's condition did not improve, but on the other hand, it did not get worse. There was that to be glad of.

It was at their local 'Well-Healed Centre' that they saw the advert for a Rebirthing Week. It promised, through its technique of circular connected natural breathing, to unlock old and sick body patterns, restore the natural flow and open the way to healing. Flowing rang up the group-leader to check out further details - the three women were by now getting all too wary of yet another Kwik-Fit solution that promised them miracles through the simple repeated pronouncement of affirmations. Phoenix, the Rebirthing therapist in charge of Breathe Free, told Flowing his breathing techniques concentrated on getting people back to the moment of first breath. Hot water tubs were used to simulate the warm amniotic fluid. He said that reconnecting with the first breath freed the way to total body health. The only catch seemed to be the price which at £500 per week seemed hardly in keeping with the clinic's name. However, it did all seem reassuringly bodily, maternal, womb-like and free from all the mental chatter of the mind-programmers. The three friends decided to take the plunge.

And it proved indeed to be a bit of a plunge, there were delightful tubs of warm water scented with aromatic oils and in these the Rebirthees wallowed sensuously, kitted up with snorkels with which to submerge themselves for long periods. Phoenix and his assistants strolled around the edges of the tubs, priming them as to the approved breathing-practices. Totally immersed in the liquid heat, it was easy to regress into primal peace, wafted back into the ancient ocean of creation, back into tideless waters that murmured to the primitive brain of a time before birth, before awareness of day and night, of hot and cold, joy and pain.

When not floating in the hot-tubs, the Rebirthees lay in a circle, heads touching at the centre, swaddled in blankets and breathing rhythmically together to the comforting sound of a muffled maternal heart-beat. They were given giant dummies to suck on, flavoured with comforting gels. As they breathed their way through the hours together, they experienced many strange physical sensations, wept many tears in release, shed much body-armour, and caught glimpses of life lived to the full through restoring contact with correctly breathed air. The world seemed for once a really safe and tranquil place to breathe in, to be in.

And this, they were told by the Rebirthers, was what reality was really all about. It was indeed all peace, love, and all safety ( and, of course, all prosperity. ) As the Rebirthees lay like new-born babes at their feet, the Rebirthers moved gently amongst them, murmuring soft phrases - 'I feel the peace.' 'It is now safe to love.' - into the newly attuned ears. After a few days of the lulling environment, Flowing and Maya felt indeed in a very different space from the one they had been in on their arrival. Even Marianne's illness was something that could be taken in their stride, from day to day, breathing their way through any troubling thoughts, doubts or pain, back to deep peace. Marianne, herself, seemed a little better, though quieter and more thoughtful than usual.

And then towards the end of the week, the Rebirthers began gradually to change the tempo. The placid babes were encouraged to cast aside their dummies, to start sitting up and to take notice of the world around them. The soothing dulcet flute music was replaced with bracing marching polkas and the first faltering steps were encouraged. Those who exhibited tendencies to regress to the less demanding world of dummy-sucking and the hot-tubs were gently but firmly guided towards the challenges of eating solid meals with a knife and fork. The Rebirthers were preparing them for re-emergence from the womb-like safety of the group to face the challenges of the outer world.

But before the group was to wind up, the graduating class had to be instructed in the new language of those reborn. And indeed it was a very new language, though at times vaguely reminiscent of half-heard Christian born-again revelations. Moreover, mastering the new art of living, as Phoenix began to outline it, made fire-walking seem a rather rudimentary feat. Their whole grasp of the universe was to be utterly transformed. Phoenix was to deliver the Rebirther's cosmic punchline. And all at the cut-price of £500 per head.

Working his way towards his revelation, Phoenix explained how the physical body, if adequately supplied with properly regulated doses of air and guided by wise and correct instructions from the mind, would go from strength to strength, healing itself of any ailment that beset it, and not ever succumbing to the ageing process. The physical body, powered by natural connected breathing, was a perfect temple and in reality an **immortal** vehicle for their souls!! There was thus no need for any of us to die. The life that the Reborn were to re-enter was theirs not just for a meagre three-score years and ten but for ever. Any indication to the contrary (culled from an overzealous brooding over grave-stones in morbid visits to cemeteries) was the result of distress-patterns, victim-consciousness that doomed our precious bodily temples to the unnecessary trauma of illness, ageing and the death-process. Disease itself was a turning away from our birth-right, it was underneath a rejection of the life-process, of God and the chance to live for ever, in short it was sin made visible.

Reclining totally relaxed in the Rebirthing couches, the group attempted to digest the startling new details of their eternal existence. At first there was an incredulous silence. Then this was broken by outbursts of hilarity. Mutinous murmurings broke out and one or two more forthright souls voiced ridicule of Phoenix's preposterous cast-iron certainties. Was the whole of documented human experience and the evidence of their own senses to be overturned by a simple new breathing-technique and an aura of invincibility?

Many many questions were thrown at Phoenix. But each doubt or query about the invulnerability of their bodies to the depredations of time met with the same stock responses - think immortal, be immortal - connect with your breath, to the vitality of life, and physical immortality was the prize. They were instructed to resume their new natural connected breathing, to think immortal and to be at peace. All this talk of physical death only gave it power, raised their anxiety-levels and damaged their immune systems.

In the end it became clear that Phoenix and his assistants chose not to engage in any debate that might take them on to the actual known facts of life - though it seemed that their Rebirthing Guru and re-discoverer of the ancient secret of Physical Immortality had in fact died recently. The way the Rebirthers saw this uncomfortable detail was that he had chosen to leave his physical vehicle at that particular point to further his work from the etheric realm. Nothing ruffled their profoundly peaceful exteriors.

The group was softly but firmly instructed to resume slow connected breathing. Soothing music was put on the sound-system. The Rebirthers lead some slow hypnotic peace chants. Within half an hour the worrying turmoil of questions had been replaced. People were beginning to loosen up again, get out of head-spaces and go with the peace and bliss of the body. It was time for the Closing Circle.

Phoenix and his assistants ushered them all into a circle of candles which had been lovingly prepared amidst a fragrant shower of flowers. The rebirthing process was to be finally completed with a ceremony, a ceremony that was to sever the umbilical cord that tied them to the mother. But firstly, in deference to the queries that some of them had raised, and now that they were all in a more centred space, there was time for a short final question and answer session, to clear up any last lingering doubts.

It seemed, however, that there were none. A

peaceful silence reigned. This was eventually broken by a tentative last-minute query from a quietly-spoken young woman. She voiced fears as to whether it was going to be as entirely safe out there as the Rebirthers had portrayed it. She had, she bravely revealed to them all, been grossly and violently raped and she still did not feel, even after the week's tranquil shelter, entirely safe to love. Phoenix turned reassuringly towards her. 'You must lay aside your fear' he stated. 'Fear attracts negative energies towards it. Have instead compassion. There is only one more thing that can be said on this. Imagine the violation the rapist must feel to have committed such an act.'

The silence deepened. Finally, a rather thin-looking man confessed that, although he felt much better for the week's therapy, he was worried lest the diabetes, from which he had suffered all his life, should recur. Phoenix in reply reminded him gently that any sickness was a turning-away from God, that it was up to each one of us whether or not we chose to be healthy. He then consulted a tome well-loved by the Rebirthers entitled 'It's So Sick To Be Sick.' It informed him that diabetes was caused by holding on to petty jealousies and was to be overcome by cultivating a more giving approach to others. Phoenix then suggested that donating money to himself for new hot-tubs would be an example of a restorative action for the illness in question. Phoenix's second response was also received in peaceful silence, punctuated only by the quiet rhythmic flow of collective connected breathing. It seemed there were no further questions.

So now at last to the final ceremony. Each group member was given a long piece of coloured thread which was attached to the centre of the circle and which they then had to tie round their waists. This created a gay wheel symbolising, they were told, the web of life. They were then to take it in turn to go round the circle, each calling out their names and affirming their ongoing connection with the centre but also their separateness as individuals. To enact the latter they were in turn to cut their cords with a silver knife, consecrated for the purpose. Then they were to pronounce their commitment to physical immortality with the statement 'I honour my physical body which is immortal.'

All went well for the first three-quarters of an hour. Without hesitation, Reborn after Reborn followed instructions, cutting the thread that bound them to the centre and pledging their commitment to an immortal frame. The circle was nearing completion. Only the three friends were left. There was a restless stirring of feet. Everyone was waiting for Marianne. She seemed lost in thought. The pause passed from the stage of pregnancy to one of barely concealed impatience over an overdue delivery. Phoenix was just about to issue Marianne with a testy prompt, when she duly pronounced her name.

But the pronouncements she made subsequently fell somewhat short of Phoenix's requirements. 'I'm Marianne, I'm 63 and really getting quite old. My muscles are beginning to sag, my skin is wrinkling, my knees are stiffening.' She demonstrated with a convincing creak. Phoenix was beginning to look a little edgy. 'But none of this need to be any more' he prompted.

Marianne continued as if she had not heard him. 'Moreover' she said next 'like others of my age, I am prey to illness, in my case, one that often ends in death.' She pulled up her sleeve and showed a nasty purple blotch on her arm. ' I may not have long to live now. And throughout this week I have been thinking about this and feeling about it.' Phoenix, at first aghast, now began to look positively militaristic. He took a step towards Marianne. She met his hostile gaze without a flinch. 'My body looks to me like a beautiful old tree, ageing and waning, queen of the forest, beginning to crack and getting ready to fall.'

Her voice was steady and brooked no interruption. She continued, this time directly to Phoenix. 'You want me to honour being young, healthy and beautiful. This I do. But I also want to honour being an old woman, being beautiful in being old, and being in the process of dying. I do not want you to try to sweep me as I am now, my ageing body, my illness, and my probable impending death, under the carpet.' She gently severed by hand the thread which connected her to the centre. 'Finally' she concluded 'I think it is totally irresponsible of you not to acknowledge the lack of safety outside for this young woman here.'

Phoenix now had the menacing vibe of a B52 bomber gliding out of its hangar, cold, angular and poised to strike. 'I think, Marianne, that you could well benefit from another week of connected breathing. Your illness could very well be linked with judgemental attitudes' was, however, all he said. 'Now for you, Flowing.' His placid mask returned.

But Flowing was not ready to speak. All that week she had been experiencing peace, safety and the chance of a future without fear. It had at the time seemed a genuine peace and built to last. But witnessing Marianne's summary rejection of Physical Immortalism threw her into terrible anxiety. She now did not know what to think or what to feel. The silence lengthened and now felt anything but peaceful.

It was then that Flowing found her voice. 'I honour my friend Marianne just as she is. I do not see her acceptance of a possible early death as a turning away from God. Rather I will love her and respect her for her ready acceptance of life and life's end.'

It was the most profound thing Flowing had ever felt or said in her life. Tears ran down her cheeks freely. And having spoken she felt her sense of peace return but this time it felt built on a firm bedrock.

Suddenly the pain, that had resided deep in her heart so long of late, lifted. She felt true to herself at last. And she had true friends. 'I second Marianne and Flowing' Maya finished the circle.

# CHAPTER 8
## CHAPTER THE LAST - OR IS IT?

Hello, readers, this is Flowing - except now I'm back to Linda, the name my mother gave me, an old goddess name, I now realise. Well, facing the grim reality of Marianne's possible death, I want to drop my tongue-in cheek humour at this point. And though you have been reading of my misadventures over the last few chapters, I don't suppose you have got much of a feel about me as a character. I wouldn't blame you all for seeing me as an ultra-gullible self-seeker. And I can only say as excuse that I wasn't really feeling me either. This is why I wrote my account so far in the third person. I'm going to write this chapter as me, and might find this hard, but here goes.

Well, the Rebirthing group was the bitter end for the three of us of our involvement in the New Age scene. I'm afraid it took the extremes of preposterousness to bring us to our senses. A sin to be sick, indeed! We have met so many women recently who are seriously ill and really made to feel guilty failures about their illnesses by the likes of Phoenix. He, incidentally, must have been dimly sentient that he had grossly mishandled Marianne's illness as he offered us all places on his next workshop at half-price. Needless to say, we didn't take him up on it.

In the weeks since then, Maya - who has also reclaimed her original name of Diana - and myself have been looking after Marianne. We've brought a comfortable old bus that just about goes and we are travelling from place to place till we find somewhere to settle. Some days, when Marianne is too ill, we have to stay put. She does go up and down a lot and it's hard not knowing how it's going to turn out. On good days, we start to think she's got it beat, but then bad days take us back down again.

We've been through so much together now and naturally we've endlessly dissected how we could have got sucked into a scene which now seems so clearly anti-feminist ( and we mean by this also anti-life and includes of course our brothers). It's taken a lot of time, much anguish and in my case, a lot of self-recrimination. Diana and Marianne have been less hard on themselves and try to console me with the fact that we aren't the only ones to be taken in by the thought-programmers. It's just so painful and frustrating to keep on battling against seemingly-solid power-structures. It's only surprising that not more people succumb to an easy solution that promises personal happiness by changing one's own head, or what one eats, or the direction you lay yourself in bed at night.

And at the risk of boring you, I need to run through for myself the lessons that have become clearer for us since we have disentangled ourselves from the wheel of endless and expensive self-transformation. Much of this may be obvious but it's taken me weeks to get here so please bear with me as I spell out the insights I've gained at the end of all this. And I promise a bit of a chuckle at the end to round off my tale.

So first, I know now that true spirituality must for me embrace also collective political struggle. And that a healing lifestyle isn't just about meditation, herbs, food, Birkenstock sandals - it's also about where our money comes from, how it is distributed, how we live, who looks after the children, the needy and how - questions many New Agers often dismiss airily as if this is not what true spirituality is about. Their often dualistic either-or mindset splits the spiritual quest for a better life for us all from the political means to achieve it.

In thinking things through on this score, we have had to confront the uncomfortable fact that Diana's legacy came from some very dubious sources. We've given most of it to Women's Centres and Refuges and kept enough to keep us through Marianne's illness and set us up in a new venture. Maybe we're beginning to sound guilt-trippingly right-on. I hope not. We are, I think, just three ordinary women trying to get by, only now we're trying to find a spirituality together as women, one that is strong enough to take us through Marianne's possible death.

And we certainly now know what we don't want. We don't want a spirituality that tells us everything is fine the way it is, and that if we experience different, then there's something wrong with us, some disease called victim-consciousness. Nor a spirituality that divides bits of our lives into higher and lower, inner and outer and says e.g. only work on the inner. Again the either-or mindset.

As for the line that it is thought alone that creates reality, that feels to me very much like 'In the beginning, there was the Word, and the Word was God.' If you look at creation as we women do it, it is sometimes a bit bloody, messy and painful but it's certainly got ecstasy, power, beauty and feelings. I'm not saying that mind, or thoughts, aren't part of our way of creating because our creations aren't only children but cover all sorts of fields. But I don't want a spirituality that says creation is about one thing or aspect only, or that we as women must turn our backs on instinct, our gut-feeling, passionate love-making, bonds that partake of and give life. To embrace only Logos seems to land us shackled to a cold sterile bed of abstraction.

As for the corollary, mind over matter with all the affirmations, I don't now understand how I didn't see that affirming only one side of things is just not balanced. So in affirming that I deserve money, joy, the lot, I also need to affirm that pain is part of life, that I need to deal with it and that I can - and that poverty is a reality for many and that I must struggle in solidarity with the oppressed. As for all those exhortations not to get too attached, try telling that to the New Age leaders about their power and money. And for us women, what is wrong with passionate bonds? to our lovers? to our kids? to our earth? Underneath, the non-attachment schools shore up the life-denying positions that tell us that it is always jam tomorrow, heaven some-place else and that this earthly garden is not where it's at, so don't get too caught up in it. Or bother about trying to change society for the better.

Nor in the end is there anything at all spiritual about packaging native religions for a pretty penny, having ripped off their best land as well. Diana and I finally got round to applauding Marianne for giving the Harmonic Convergers the feedback they deserved. She saw through them way before us. She modestly claims that it was the laurels that got her wise as to what was going on there. Certainly the whole jamboree was cultural theft reaching crazy proportions - it was nearly-to-a man affluent Westerners zoning in on ancient sites, adamantly certain that it was their own god-given right to use the sacred spaces of others, no questions asked, for rituals filched without proper understanding from other times or places, the whole stitched together in a timetable/itinerary that looks like it was spawned by an over-imaginative computer gone berserk.

These New Age devotees of ancient sacred sites mostly keep themselves out of the land-rights struggles of the indigenous peoples in their battles to preserve their sacred space. And we have discovered from other women that many Harmonic Convergence groups celebrated like we did at Delphi, with the enactment of a sexual pairing of a woman with a man, the hoped-for outcome to be, yes, wait for it, yet another Divine Child (male of course). What seemed to have transpired in sad reality as the result of this hyped-up happening was that more than one unfortunate woman had to find her way to an abortion clinic when subsequent events showed the sacred marriage wasn't made in heaven, rather in the wearily predictable fantasies of male esoteric scholars.

The whole circus was the brainchild of a handful of such men who see themselves as potent channels of spirit. The Aborigines certainly didn't share their opinion and drove eager enlightened Sundancers unceremoniously away from their sacred Ayers Rock.

Well, I'm going off on a bit of a lecture here, but have only a few more things to say in this vein. It does seem fishy to me that many of the big boys in the New Age movement have moneyed backgrounds, their ventures usually prosper with very steep prices, and their Network of Light corresponds uncannily with centres of white colonial capitalism. As for THE PLAN - in my attempts to digest the dozens of highly indigestible esoteric books that are the true foundation of New Ageism, I couldn't see the wood for the trees. Amongst all the jargon of Masters guided from the etheric realms of Shamballa, of impending Luciferic initiations for all of mankind, of the pre-eminence of the Solar Logos, of the Seven Rays, blah, blah, blah.... is implanted the vision of one world religion being embraced by all of humanity, the New Age religion.

This claims to be a synthesis of the best from all traditions, but it is in reality an eclectically chosen hotchpotch that promotes the doctrine that, though we are all divine in the New Age, some are more divine than others. One of the most blatant 'new'-age package informs us that they, the Hierarchy, will come down to Earth to 'guide' the new world government that will 'emerge,' headed by their leader, the Lord Maitreya. He'll sell himself to the masses by claiming to redistribute world food-supplies fairly and by putting an end to wars. Those who don't take willingly to the new religious dispensation will, however, the Plan states clearly, suffer a 'cleansing' or 'disappear' to another planetary level - they won't be physically incarnate any longer!! Maitreya, it is claimed, will bring an end to wars. But in the event that the batteries of affirmations fail to win over hearts, he seems quite disposed to nuke dissenting groups and he is particularly hostile, it appears from the writings, to Jewish people.

So, though I have tried to make my story amusing, the underlying purpose of my tale is deadly serious - the esoteric sources for some strands of the New Age movement are similar to those of the Nazis. Moreover, behind the facade, there appears to be a cohesive and international group of New Age leaders, all over the industrialised world and elsewhere, operating in groups with misleadingly benign titles. They are financially quite strong and have already influenced sections of business to their values. The sources for other of the many divergent schools of new age 'wisdom' are often equally dubious or nebulously ascribed to the guidance or channelling of some charismatic figure who prospers from the hopeless naivety of followers.

More scaringly, they seem fond of the term Warrior and the military battalion called the First Earth Battalion, which started life as a breakaway troop of idealists, has been co-opted into activities such as psychological brainwashing and torture of prisoners held under the prevention of terrorism agenda. When it comes down to it, the New World Order they plan replaces control of the planet by one group of men with another, allegedly a superior breed of men, as they hold themselves to be operating to spiritual values. Their buzz-words sound harmless enough - manifestation, planetary citizen, global village - but I think they hope to co-opt these words, which nurture the all-too human aspirations for an interdependent outlook, for their own power-bases.

Paradoxically those who live in new age centres are often good and inspiring people who work very hard and offer venues for a few amazing pioneering radical spirits like Joanna Macy. The implication of the fact that selling spirituality and new world ways however brings internal contradictions, glaringly obvious to perceptive critics, is not even raised as a problem by new age centre-workers. They thus seems blind as to whose agenda they are actually serving. Presenting spirituality as a financial commodity is the economic back-bone of these new often 'eco' communities – new age centres are embedded in a style of living that is not otherwise financially viable. This has led to a completely undiscriminating medley of a few quality offerings with a welter of delusional drivel which feeds a hungry market of desperate souls wanting to find some distraction from a planet on the verge of total species extinction. Worried – wait, spend your money and what time you have left tracking orbs!!! - Certainly easier than taking courageous acts of hope to work to restore our shattered money-systems and the dereliction in towns and cities. The clientele of New Age spirituality is in general very well off and I know of no new age centres in destitute neighbourhoods, looking squarely at the abject face of poverty, squalor and self-destruct. It is Polyannism - not looking and thus not choosing to see, let alone to address. And the models of a new society that they are touting for all of humanity are not replicable without input from the wealthy.

For their model of change is based on the premise that we all have the power to chose and act. But these capacities are not god-given or attainable at a price from the latest glitzy workshop or by a battery of affirmations. The power to change is not simply a personal attribute, they are social acquisitions which depend on access to material resources and education. So far from repairing the damage done by society or changing the social order, the new age is at best a small irrelevance, at best a temporary comfort, at worst a deliberate distraction. And I think it is no accident that the new age enterprise was introduced in the heady days of 60's politically radical hope and action. It then fed nicely into the subsequent reactionary right–wing ideologies of the 80's which saw the backlash against communitarian approaches and a frogmarch back to individualism with a vengeance.

Who are the paymasters behind the promotion of prosperity consciousness ideologies, and the like - who benefits from selling the idea that change has to come from within, what political philosophies and structures do such ideas imply? The answer seems to me to be that they stem from reactionary philosophies and also favour hierarchical leadership. With token open governance systems on view, new age centres in general operate with non-elected boards of faceless trustees and unaccountable management groups who really pull the strings. New age culture suppresses challenge and dissent by branding critics as judgemental and/or negative. Those who persist in questioning tend to be sidelined, ignored, scapegoated or shamed. As to who benefits from new age spirituality? I can only conclude that it is the capitalistic elite who must smile benignly at the naïve claims of the devotees and probably funnel funds to ensure the future of these centres should their money manifestation falter.

Well, that's got all the heavy analysis out of the way. And this leaves me a little bit older and hopefully a little bit wiser. In looking back over the last few chapters of my life, I am sad that I let myself get carried along on a tide of self-deception. I am particularly ashamed that I even went so far as to blame my lack of money on attitudes passed on to me by my hard-pressed mother, solvable by a glib new thought-programme.

I also feel ashamed of the way I left my flat-mates without even taking time to send them a postcard to let them know that I was alright or to tell them whether I still wanted my old room. I visited them for a few days recently and went through the whole thing with them. They were really understanding. And said that my room is still there for me any time and they're glad I've seen the light (or rather had enough of it). If I do go back there to live, I'll certainly re-instate my political posters. But I'll keep my soul-stirring landscapes up too. Perhaps my vulnerability to New Ageism occurred because I had just got too burnt-out being a 'politico' who didn't take enough time to relax, unwind and generally look after herself.

Meanwhile, where to from here? Well, while she is so ill, Diana and I are sticking with Marianne. The fact that she has cancer of the blood has made us consider what is a healthy blood-bond for women. Marianne's illness has got little, if anything, to do with her thoughts and is probably due to the chemical and radio-active overload that besieges the earth. And not once in our New Age capers, with their disembodied Full Moon invocations, was there any mention made of the connection between the moon's cycles and women's menstrual power. And in the end that is where we conclude our spirituality must be rooted – in our bodies and their cycles, in the earth and her cycles, our connections to each other and to the web of life. And about restoring our shattered communities around values, not of self-blaming philosophies and batteries of affirmations, but of compassion grounded in practical support and care, and community sharing of the joys and griefs so entwined in the living of the Mystery. We are truly all in this together.

For our brothers in their quest we can only pray that the lure of power and money that patriarchal spiritualities offer them does not blind them further to the essential umbilical bond to us, that our welfare and theirs must be one. And they can find a spirituality kindred to ours that marries them to the earth.

And now I would like to leave you all with a happy ending - but I feel our story is still in the making. And though the omens look grim at the moment, we are hoping that we aren't in for another 'cleansing', that the Burning Times aren't going to be repeated on a global scale and that there can be good times for women again.

But laughter is the best medicine in my book so I end with a bit of a chuckle. Here's a list of just a few of the New Age books and workshops that we have dubbed with our official psychic health warning:

* 'The Art of Creative Necrophilia' by Lovem N. Leavem.

* 'Transmissions from the Akashic Records' as channelled by Alice Comet Bailey - How to Bore your Way to Higher Consciousness.

* 'Guilt Without Sex' by Elektra Fied.

* 'How to Wing Your Way to Self-confidence through Denial, Narcissism and Ostentation' by B.A. Winna.

* 'The Joys of Photophilia' by David Razzle Dazzle Spangle.

* 'The Sacred Cow of the Horned God' (as learnt from women) by John my Ex-wife Has All the Problems

Mountain Ash.

* 'Great Earth Mysteries Made Even More Mysterious' by the Moots of Male Magicians, Ley Hunters and Wizards, Inc.

* 'Unconditional Screwing - oops, - Unconditional Loving' by John Zipper.

* 'How to Join the Great White Brotherhood' promoted by Ariel and Radiant.

* 'The Art of 20th Century Dying - Vibrate Your Atoms the Windscale Way' with gift-offer of holiday in specially bombarded graveyard-site to speed up your exit.

* 'Total Orgasm Through Alfalfa Sprouts.'
* 'Cosmic Unconsciousness Made Easy - How to Tune Out Wars, Famines and Disasters.'
*'Experiencing the Creative Ecstasy of Wisdom Tooth Extraction.'
 * 'Great Peace of Mind through a Great Piece of the Cake' by X.Tortion.